FROM LUTHER TO 1580:
A PICTORIAL ACCOUNT

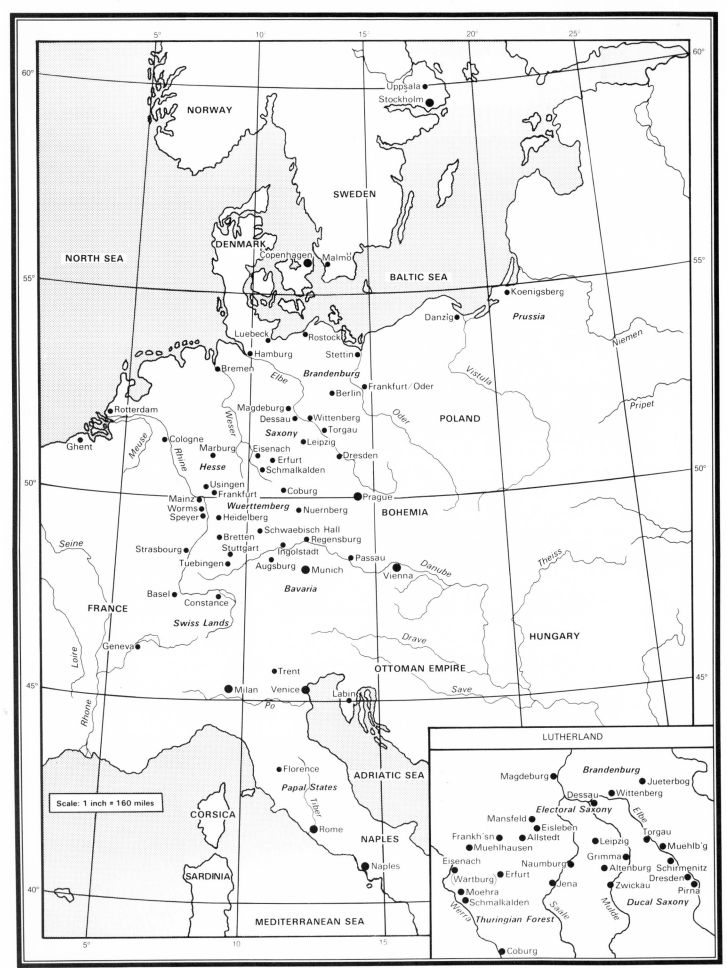

REFERENCE MAP OF CENTRAL EUROPE IN THE TIME OF THE REFORMATION

Map by Erwin Weber

FROM Luther TO 1580

A PICTORIAL ACCOUNT

PLACES, PERSONS, AND EVENTS
LEADING TO THE BOOK OF CONCORD

by Erwin Weber

TEXT BY INGETRAUT LUDOLPHY

Preface by Conrad Bergendoff

Publishing House
St. Louis

Dedicated to my family,
my wife Barbara and my two sons Walter and Kurt

FRONT COVER:
The lamp may be used in connection with the
Reformation as a symbol of every Christian's
search for knowledge of the truth.

Design by Edward Luhmann

Concordia Publishing House, St. Louis Missouri
Copyright © 1977 Concordia Publishing House

The Scripture quotations in this publication
are from the Revised Standard Version
of the Bible,
copyrighted 1946, 1952, © 1971, 1973

MANUFACTURED IN THE UNITED STATES OF AMERICA

Library of Congress Cataloging in Publication Data

Weber, Erwin, 1921-
    From Luther to 1580.

    1. Lutheran Church—History—Pictorial works.
2. Luther, Martin, 1483-1546—Portraits, etc.
3. Lutheran in Germany—Portraits. I. Title.
BX8018.W42   284′.1′09   76-58401
ISBN 0-570-03264-4

PREFACE

The one hundred years between 1480 and 1580 were of profound significance in the history of the Christian church. From Moehra, the village of Luther's ancestral home, and from the Diet of Augsburg, which gave rise to the Augsburg Confession (the Augustana), to the publication of *The Book of Concord,* which became the confessional basis of Lutheran churches all over the world, scores of important personalities and numerous cities and buildings became associated with events of world history.

Professor Erwin Weber has made it his goal to give the modern visitor to the lands of the Reformation an authentic guidebook in the form of pictures and accompanying narrative. In a graphic way we can follow Luther's career through the area of his activity and into countries where his followers instituted lasting reforms. When we see the places and the people as they appeared to Luther's contemporaries, we ourselves become participants in the great drama.

This volume is remarkable in that the text Professor Weber has chosen to translate is the work of an author today living, writing, and doing research in Luther's native territory, known as Lutherland.

In these years of the quadricentennial of *The Book of Concord* this valuable book can truly aid us in celebrating events of such enduring importance.

Conrad Bergendoff

AETHERNA IPSE SVAE MENTIS SIMVLACHRA LVTHERVS
EXPRIMIT·AT VVLTVS CERA LVCAE OCCIDVOS.

·M·D·X·X·

Luther as a monk. Engraving by Lucas Cranach the Elder, 1520. (Lutherhalle, Wittenberg)

INTRODUCTION

Many books have been published dealing with the life and work of Martin Luther. Often the text, though lengthy, ends with the death of the Great Reformer. This illustrated book deals not only with the life of Luther but also with the spread of the Reformation and the schisms that threatened to split the Evangelical Lutheran Church after Luther's death. Furthermore, it deals with the search for unity, culminating in the publication of *The Book of Concord* in 1580.

An attempt is made in this book to illustrate the years from 1480 to 1580 with a minimum of text and a maximum of pictures. It is my hope that the reader may become better acquainted with the important events, places, and people of the Reformation period. Although attempts have been made to show that the Reformation of the 16th century was a result of various economic, political, and social forces, in its very beginning it was purely an ecclesiastical movement, rooting itself solely in the theological development of its leader, Martin Luther.

As we approach the 400th anniversary of the publication of *The Book of Concord*, this book will hopefully illustrate that the Reformation was accomplished by more than just a few individuals during this period of complexity, faith, and human failings. For in the final analysis, this book is a pedagogical undertaking. It is my hope that the numerous photographs, coupled with the short narrative, will bring Lutherans in all lands closer to one another, when they have seen the common historical origins of their churches.

This book would not have been possible without the help and assistance I received from my colleagues at Augustana College and the guidance from many a theologian and church historian in this country and abroad. I am especially indebted to Dr. Ingetraut Ludolphy for not only writing the original text for this book but also editing the English version of the translation. I also wish to thank Dr. George Forell for his helpful advice and Dr. Conrad Bergendoff for his encouragement and assistance throughout this project. Finally, I want to thank the government of the German Democratic Republic for the cooperation I received in gathering material for this book. I am also deeply indebted to Klaus G. Beyer in Weimar for his friendship and kindness. Of the 171 pictures in this book, 29 were contributed by this famous artist with a camera who in May 1976 was the first photographer in the German Democratic Republic to be honored with the *Kunstpreis der DDR* for his creative achievements. Thus it is my hope that this book will show not only the beauty of Lutherland but other regions covered in this work of love.

Erwin Weber

CONTENTS

Events Illustrated

I. Luther's Ancestral Home and Early Years, 1480–1505

1480

Moehra, Luther's Ancestral Home   **Plates 1—4**

Martin Luther's parents came from Moehra, a village located at the edge of the Thuringian Forest about nine miles south of the Wartburg castle—the castle which was later to attain great importance for Luther and thereby significance for the Reformation. The farming community of Moehra at that time belonged to Elector Ernest of Saxony, the father of Frederick the Wise. Elector Ernest only rarely interfered in the affairs of the self-governing administration of the village. The peasants were relatively independent.

Heine Luder, the head of the family and grandfather of Martin Luther, was certainly in the village of Moehra around 1480. Since the father, Hans Luder, was the oldest son, he could not inherit the family estate.[1] Therefore he became a miner, at the latest by the time of Martin's birth. The copper mines of the county of Mansfeld in nearby Saxony attracted many an ambitious young man at that time. At first Martin Luther's parents found a place to live in Eisleben. The economic opportunities in Eisleben were apparently not great enough, so the family moved to Mansfeld in the early summer of 1484. In the beginning the father was presumably a simple miner, but already before 1491 he joined one of the many small unions of the community of miners which facilitated the organization of work. At the same time he leased, together with another person from Mansfeld, a small smelting works (foundry), so that he could keep himself and his growing family on a financially sound basis. Hans Luder had to work hard, and although his standard of living improved somewhat, he never became rich or affluent. Work and worry are etched deeply into the faces of Luther's parents as portrayed by Cranach the Elder. Martin Luther is considered to resemble his mother. The sensibleness that characterizes the picture of Luther as a monk can also be seen in the painting of Luther's mother. In the face of the father we can see the vigor he employed to better himself economically and socially, and with which he also resisted his son when the latter sacrificed honor and wealth to enter a monastery. His father had planned a career as a lawyer for his son, and a marriage which would have been favorable for the Luther family.

Luther was indebted to both of his parents for the strict upbringing which was the custom of those days. Because he took a nut one day, little Martin was beaten so badly by his mother that the blood flowed. Luther's father was just as strict. The piety in that home reflected the times wherein erroneous ideas and superstitions were mingled with Christian belief. A special patron saint of the miners was St. Anna, who was said to be the mother of the Virgin Mary.

1483

Eisleben, Luther's Place of Birth   Plates 5—8

Luther was born in Eisleben on Nov. 10, 1483, as the second son of the family. He received the name Martin because he was baptized on Nov. 11, the Feast of St. Martin. Luther had several brothers and sisters, but unfortunately we know very little about them.

1484

Move to Mansfeld and First School   Plates 9—12

Martin spent his earliest childhood in Mansfeld, where he was probably attending the city school by March 1488. There he learned reading, writing, singing, and Latin, under strict discipline. Singing was taught so that the pupils could participate in the services of the church. Latin was at that time the language of the administrators and educated people. One had to master this language in order to have an opportunity for an advanced career. This medieval, everyday Latin was considered coarse and rude by the Humanists. To be sure, Luther never wrote the elegant Latin of the Humanists, in which his friend and co-worker Melanchthon was an expert, but Luther's Latin had a clear and fluid quality.

While attending school in Mansfeld, Luther certainly became familiar with the three usual texts taught in class: stories by Pseudo-Cato, Aesop, and Terence.[2] The humor expressed in these works transmitted wisdom for life in addition to the teaching of the traditional grammar.

The dukes of Mansfeld, who had their castle on a hill overlooking the city, would later play a role during the last days of Luther. In order to settle a disagreement of a purely secular nature between the dukes, Luther traveled to Eisleben in December 1545 and once again at the end of January 1546. After he succeeded in settling the argument, Luther died in the city of his birth on Feb. 18, 1546.

1497

Magdeburg, "Brothers of the Common Life"   Plates 13—15

Luther attended school one year in Magdeburg on the Elbe River, beginning in the spring of 1497. The school was run by the Brothers of the Common Life, an order founded in the Netherlands. In these famous schools the Brothers emphasized reading the Holy Scriptures, heartfelt piety, and a return to the simple life. Here in Magdeburg, as later in Eisenach, Luther supported himself by being a member of a small school chorus which went from house to house singing songs. At that time this manner of earning a living was considered neither degrading nor a sign of poverty.

Luther later in life described a moving experience in meeting a

Franciscan monk, the former Prince William of Anhalt: "He had so fasted, neglected, and mortified his body that he looked like a dead man, only skin and bones, he died soon after that.... Whoever looked at him was deeply moved and had to feel ashamed of his own secular position in life." Even after 35 years, in 1533, Luther gave this vivid account of the incident in Magdeburg.

1498

Change of School to Eisenach   Plates 16—18

In 1498 Luther was sent by his parents to Eisenach. This became his beloved city, for which he always had a tender spot in his heart. He attended the *Pfarrschule,* the parish school of St. George, where he developed an admiration for his teachers. He soon found a place to eat with a pious, distinguished, well-to-do lady, who had enjoyed his singing and devout praying in church. This lady was probably the wife of a prosperous businessman, Heinrich Schalbe, but whether Luther lived here or with the Cottas, who were related to the Schalbes, or at another place in Eisenach, is not known for certain. Nevertheless, through these families Luther came into a circle of people in which religion was the most important part of their lives.

1501

University Studies Begin in Erfurt   Plates 19—26

At the end of April 1501, Luther began his studies at the University of Erfurt. As prescribed, he enrolled first in the College of Liberal Arts, where the seven courses of the *artes liberales* were taught. These courses had little to do with what we understand as the term "arts" today. They included the *trivium,* which were courses in grammar, dialectic, and rhetoric, as well as the *quadrivium,* which included courses in geometry, mathematics, music, and astronomy. At the end of the Middle Ages the studies of the *trivium* gave the student a solid foundation in the Latin language. The studies in the *quadrivium* were the beginnings of our modern science, but at the time of Luther only "natural philosophy" was taught. It included a few facts of a scientific nature.

We know two of Luther's teachers from this time in Erfurt: Bartholomaeus Arnoldi, called Usingen, from Usingen in Nassau,[3] and Jodocus Trutvetter from Eisenach. Both were theologians representing the dominant philosophy of the school, that of William Ockham.

After a student had successfully completed three years in the College of Liberal Arts, he was permitted to attend one of the graduate schools in theology, law, or medicine. As a graduate student, he could teach in the College of Liberal Arts.

Luther lived in the *Georgenburse* in Erfurt. A *Burse* was a house for students, with strict regulations. The entire day of the student, as well as his studies, were carefully supervised by a faculty member with the rank of master. It was mandatory that the student attend classes each day, offer daily prayers, and attend religious services. There were hours set aside each day for review under the direction of the faculty member supervising the *Burse.* Besides, a professor from the university would send a topic for debate each week.

Numerous such topics, which Luther later compiled for his students, have been preserved to this day. In debating a topic, the student was required to answer his opponent as quickly, skillfully, and irrefutably as possible. Material for the debate had to be prepared in advance, including quotations from literature. The exercise was used to train the student's memory, his logic, and his ability to respond effectively and skillfully. It was a method of formal education that the student had to defend a topic which did not originate with him and with which he might not agree. How excellently Luther had made use of this kind of a formal education shows later in the debate in Leipzig, where it was reported: "Luther is extremely well educated. Above all, he possesses an astounding knowledge of the Bible, as if he had memorized almost all of it. . . . He is never at a loss for words, because he has such a tremendous vocabulary."

At Erfurt Luther was unconsciously immersed in the spirit of Ockhamism. But it was not until later that he recognized his agreement with this philosophy, which considered reason incapable of explaining the mysteries of belief. Ockhamism belonged to the philosophical school of Nominalism, which considered only the individual thing (a particular experience) as real, not the general term (the idea). Therefore access to another world was for the nominalists only possible through revelation. Subsequently, Luther rejected the nominalists' emphasis on man's free will as well as on the inherent goodness in man. He also did not like nominalist devotion to the "old heathen," Aristotle, in spite of the fact that Luther was indebted to him for much scientific knowledge.

Although Luther, inspired by Usingen and Trutvetter, became acquainted with the works of other classical authors, such as Ovid, Virgil, and Plautus, he displayed no real connection with Humanism until a much later time.

PLATE 1. Luther's ancestral home in the village of Moehra. The home is not the original. A new one was built in its place in 1618. The statue of Luther, and similar ones located in other Luther cities, were erected in the middle of the 19th century.

PLATE 2. Luther's father Hans. Painting by Lucas Cranach the Elder, 1527. (Wartburg-Stiftung, Eisenach)

PLATE 3. Luther's mother Margarethe. Painting by Lucas Cranach the Elder, 1527. (Wartburg-Stiftung, Eisenach)

PLATE 4. Village street in present-day Moehra, a farm community. View from the ancestral home of the Luther family. Descendants of the Luther family are farmers and are still living in Moehra to this day.

PLATE 5. City of Eisleben. View from the tower of St. Andrew's Church. Luther was baptized on Nov. 11, 1483, in the St. Peter and Paul's Church, at the right.

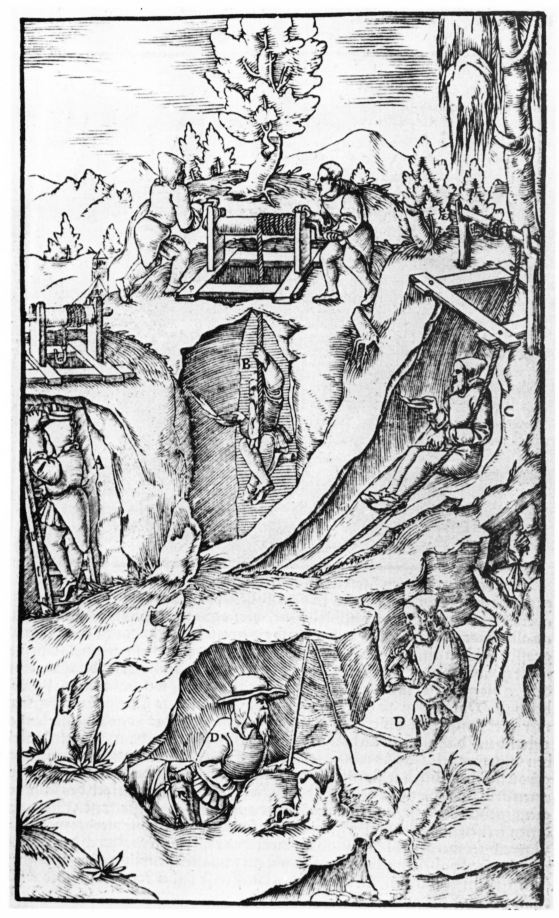

PLATE 6. The miners of the 16th century. Woodcut by Rudolf Deutsch and others from the book by George Agricola, *Vom Bergwerk*, Basel, 1557. (Universitaetsbibliothek, Karl-Marx-Universitaet, Leipzig)

PLATE 7. The house in which Luther was born on Nov. 10, 1483, in Eisleben. View from the courtyard. The building was reconstructed in 1693 and 1819.

PLATE 8. Digging the ore out of the ground. Woodcut by Rudolf Deutsch and others from the book by George Agricola, *Vom Bergwerk*, 1557. (Universitaetsbibliothek, Karl-Marx-Universitaet, Leipzig)

PLATE 9. City of Mansfeld. View from the former castle of the counts of Mansfeld. The school which Luther attended is located next to the church. Luther's father's house can be seen on the right.

PLATE 10. Luther's father's house in Mansfeld. View from the courtyard. This house is not the original, a new one was built in its place at the beginning of the 18th century.

PLATE 11. The former castle of the counts of Mansfeld. View from the courtyard toward the ornate gate of the tower. The gate is attributed to Ludwig Binder, 1518.

PLATE 12. St. Anna, patron saint of the miners. Lindenwood sculpture by an unknown artist from Otterwisch near Leipzig around 1530. (Museum fuer Geschichte der Stadt Leipzig)

PLATE 13. Magdeburg on the Elbe River. View toward the cathedral from the west. Adjacent to the cathedral are the buildings of the former cathedral school, which Luther did not attend but later had contacts with it.

PLATE 14. Detail of the romanesque structure of the former cathedral school, dating back to the beginning of the 12th century. The school which Luther attended was located in another section of the city.

PLATE 15. Death with Scythe and Hour Glass. A water color in the Student Registration Book No. II, 1498—1600, of the University of Erfurt. (Stadtarchiv, Erfurt)

PLATE 16. City of Eisenach. View toward the romanesque structure of St. Nicholas Church and the city gate through which Luther undoubtedly walked when he came to this city in 1498.

PLATE 17. Luther or Cotta House in Eisenach. Luther is said to have lived in this elegant half-timbered-style building. It was destroyed during World War II and now is completely rebuilt.

PLATE 18. The church school of St. George in Eisenach which Luther attended. View from the inner courtyard toward the gothic-style walls of the former church school.

PLATE 19. City of Erfurt. View toward the cathedral in which Luther was ordained to the priesthood on April 4, 1507.

PLATE 20. Luther's name is recorded in the Student Registration Book No. II, 1498—1600, of the University of Erfurt: "Martinus Luder de Mansfelt." (Stadtarchiv, Erfurt)

PLATE 21. A building of the former University of Erfurt, *Collegium maius,* before its destruction in World War II. It has not been rebuilt.

PLATE 22. Coat of arms of Crotus Rubinus surrounded by those of other famous humanists, including the one of Luther, upper left, from the Student Registration Book No. II, 1498—1600, of the University of Erfurt. (Stadtarchiv, Erfurt)

PLATE 23. As a student Luther lived in this part of the city of Erfurt. Behind the building at the left was located the *Georgenburse*, a building for students of the university.

PLATE 24. Jodocus Trutvetter, one of Luther's professors at the University of Erfurt. From the Student Registration Book No. II, 1498—1600, of the University of Erfurt. (Stadtarchiv, Erfurt)

PLATE 25. An old part of the city of Erfurt called *Kraemerbruecke.* As a monk, Luther is said to have begged here for alms, going from house to house. View from the north.

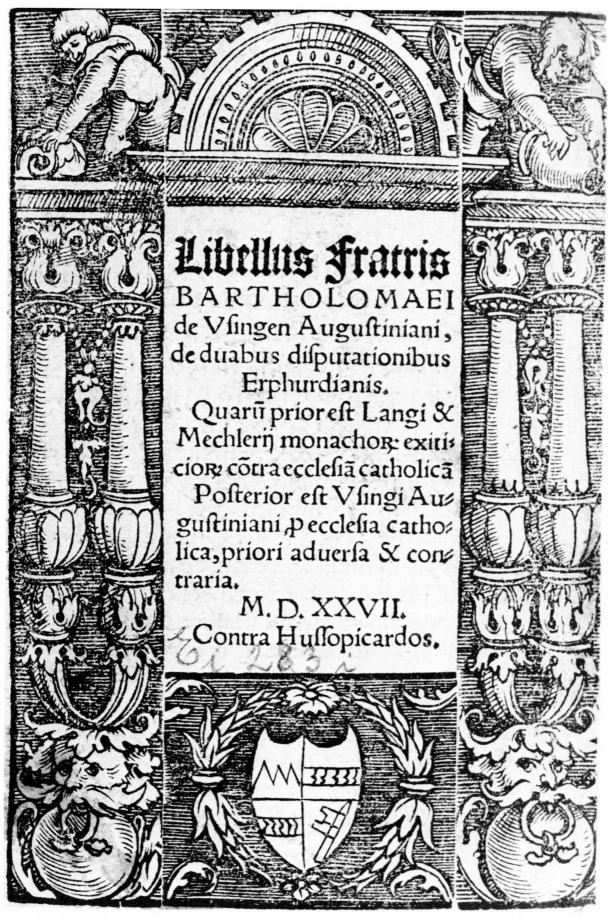

Libellus Fratris

BARTHOLOMAEI
de Vsingen Augustiniani,
de duabus disputationibus
Erphurdianis.
Quarū prior est Langi &
Mechlerij monachoꝛ exiti-
cioꝛ cōtra ecclesiā catholicā
Posterior est Vsingi Au-
gustiniani ꝑ ecclesia catholica, priori aduersa & con-
traria.

M. D. XXVII.
Contra Hussopicardos.

PLATE 26. A writing by Bartholomaeus von Usingen, one of Luther's professors at the University of Erfurt. The writing was published in 1527. (Wissenschaftliche Allgemeinbibliothek, Erfurt)

II. Luther's Monastic and University Life, 1505–1517

1505
Lightning Strikes at Stotternheim

Plate 27

Luther had hardly completed his examination for the master's degree in the beginning of February 1505 and begun to study law in May according to the wishes of his father, when he went home to his parents in Mansfeld about the 20th of June. We don't know why he left for home in the middle of the semester. Upon his return to the university, he was caught in a thunderstorm on July 2 near Stotternheim, a village located about four miles north of Erfurt. A bolt of lightening struck so close to him that he was thrown to the ground. Seized with fear, Luther called to the patron saint for such a case: "Help me, St. Anna, I will become a monk!" This event was the catalyst for Luther's entry into the monastery. We do not know the cause that drove him into monastic life. Perhaps the philosophy of Ockhamism could have played a role here, for it, to be sure, emphasized God's absolute power, majesty, and freedom, but it gives man the freedom of will and the possibility to make himself acceptable and favorable in the eyes of God by doing good works.

1505
Entry into the Monastery

Plates 28—34

On July 17, 1505, the gate of the monastery of the Augustinian Order of Hermits closed behind Luther. He had intentionally chosen this branch of the Augustinian Order since it was the strictest among the six monasteries in Erfurt.[4]

At first he was received in the *Herberge,* or hospice for guests of the monastery. He became a novice in the beginning of September. During Luther's first period in the monastery it was a time of reflection and soul-searching, not only for him but also for those in the monastery, who wanted to test the seriousness of the one who recently entered its gates. Naturally, it was a difficult time for him even without being subjected to special kinds of degradation. A year later Luther took the three monastic vows of poverty, chastity, and obedience.

Thereupon he prepared himself for ordination to the priesthood, which took place in the cathedral at Erfurt on April 4, 1507. Luther invited his father for the celebration of his first mass, which took place in the monastery church on Sunday, May 2, 1507. Luther's father came, and although he still did not agree with the steps his son had taken, he was reconciled to his son. With a heavy heart he accepted Martin's new station in life at that time.

Luther now had to turn to the study of theology. Together with his friend and fellow monk John Lang, he completed the studies, which included not only those at the university but also the so-called general studies of his order in the monastery. Now, too, Luther remained within the sphere of Ockhamistic influence.

1508

Professor in the College of Liberal Arts, Wittenberg Plates 35—43

In the fall of 1508, the monk Martin Luther received the directive to take over the professorship in moral philosophy in the College of Liberal Arts at the University of Wittenberg. This university had been founded by the elector of Saxony, Frederick the Wise, in 1502. Its first rector, or president, was Polich von Mellerstadt. He was professor of medicine and at the same time was the personal physician of the elector and later was active in the Colleges of Law and Theology. Frederick obtained for the

44

College of Theology John Staupitz, the general vicar of the Saxon Congregation of the Augustinian Order of Hermits, and at a later date, Jodocus Trutvetter, Andreas Carlstadt, and Nicholas von Amsdorf.

It is surprising that a university was established in a town with a population of a mere 2,000 inhabitants. Luther said later that the people in Wittenberg were located at the very edge of civilization. Nonetheless, in rural electoral Saxony Wittenberg was a comparatively strong fortress at the Elbe River and was situated at the crossroads of two important commercial routes so that it was an important community. Besides, Wittenberg and its surrounding area enjoyed electoral dignity by virtue of being under the sovereignty of the Saxon elector. Finally, Elector Frederick wanted to have a university in his territory because the University of Leipzig became part of ducal Saxony when Saxony was divided into the Albertine, or ducal Saxony, and Ernestine, electoral Saxony, in 1485.

Frederick loved his newly founded university very much, even if it appeared quite primitive in the beginning. There were hardly more than 300 students in the city when Luther arrived in the winter of 1508. When in subsequent years the reformers attracted many pupils to Wittenberg, consideration for the university played a definite role in the protection of Luther by the sovereign of electoral Saxony.

Probably for economic reasons, 12 of the 22 professors at the university were paid by the benefice of the All-Saints Foundation, to which belonged the reconstructed Castle Church with its gigantic relic collection. This was displayed from time to time and Frederick had invested heavily in it. Three professorships needed to be filled at the university by the two monasteries in Wittenberg. One was to be filled by the Franciscan monastery, the other two by the so-called "Black Monastery" of the Augustinian Order of Hermits. More correctly, it should be called the monastery of the "black monks," because they wore black habits on the streets. Of the two professorships available at the "Black Monastery," one was filled by Luther as professor of moral philosophy, and the other was the position of professor of Bible in the College of Theology. This post had been filled by John Staupitz since the founding of the university, but he was not able to complete his duties of lecturing because he was overloaded with assignments from his order. A more intimate connection between Luther and Staupitz probably did not exist as yet.

Luther had a considerable amount of work in Wittenberg. He had to give lectures, lead student debates and carry on his duties of his order, for example, inspecting and visiting eleven monasteries. Besides all of this he continued his education in theology.

1509
Return to Erfurt   Plates 44—45

Luther returned to Erfurt in 1509 and began to give theological lectures to a few fellow monks.[5] These lectures were based on the *Sentences* by Peter Lombard (ca. 1100—60), *Sententiarium Libri Quatuor,* a dogmatic work by the 12th-century Parisian bishop. The Sentences had been used for centuries as the basic text for lectures in theology. Luther's marginal notes in the copies, which he used for the preparation of his lectures, have been preserved and give us an opportunity to look over the shoulders of the young professor, as he worked diligently, intensely, and critically.

Here he also studied the writings of the fifth-century church father, Augustine of Hippo, who was to become important in his own theological development. Besides that, he began to learn Hebrew; but the result of his study was minimal, since Reuchlin's Grammar on the language was an insufficient text. We don't know when Luther began to occupy himself with the Greek language.

1510–1511
Journey to Rome   Plate 46

Luther's trip to Rome took place during this time in Erfurt. The exact date is not definitely known. Did the trip occur in the winter of 1510—11, or did it occur a year later? The cause was a controversial question of organization within Luther's order, behind which, however, lay theological motives.[6] The final decision was to be made by the general prior of the order. Of the two monks who had to journey to Rome, Luther, the 27- or 28-year-old, was perhaps only the *itinerarius,* that is, the associate of the *litis procurator,* or the man in charge of the mission.

Luther was certainly happy to make the trip, aside from the fact that he had taken the vow of obedience. He had the opportunity to make general confessions at the sacred shrines in Rome and to obtain indulgences, which were readily available. It is informative that with his intensive search for salvation his eyes were closed to the corruption of the church, which often enough came to light at that time in Rome. Not until later as he recalled many of these experiences did he recognize the meanings to which he had at first been blind.

Perhaps the trip to Rome had a meaning for his spiritual development, in that it failed to quiet his demands to be freed from his misery within. Luther's stay in the monastery was with great inner distress. Perhaps it had originally driven him into monastic life. Certainly he did not constantly live under this strain, but did endure moments of terrible agony. We do not know precisely what his torments were, though Luther described them to us in his *Resolutions,* or *Explanations of the Ninety-five Theses,* written in 1518 to clarify the 95 Theses, as follows:

> I myself "knew a man" (II Cor. 12:2) who claimed that he had often suffered these punishments, in fact over a very brief period of time. Yet they were so great and so much like hell that no tongue could adequately express them, no pen could describe them, and one who had not himself experienced them could not believe them. And so great were they that, if they had been sustained or had lasted for half an hour, even for one tenth of an hour, he would have perished completely and all of his bones would have been reduced to ashes. At such a time God seems terribly angry, and with him the whole creation. At such a time there is no flight, no comfort, within or without, but all things accuse. At such a time as that the Psalmist mourns, "I am cut off from thy sight" (Cf. Ps. 31:22), or at least he does not dare to say, "O Lord . . . do not chasten me in thy wrath" (Ps. 6:1). In this moment (strange to say) the soul

cannot believe that it can ever be redeemed other than that the punishment is not yet completely felt. Yet the soul is eternal and is not able to think of itself as being temporal. All that remains is the stark-naked desire for help and a terrible groaning, but it does not know where to turn for help. In this instance the person is stretched out with Christ so that all his bones may be counted, and every corner of the soul is filled with the greatest bitterness, dread, trembling, and sorrow in such a manner that all these last forever. [*Luther's Works,* Vol. 31 (Philadelphia: Muhlenberg Press, 1957), p. 129]

It is certain that his spiritual exercises in the monastery did not give him peace of mind. Ockhamism enhanced greatly his fear of being cast aside by God. God in His majesty had the freedom through His omnipotence to choose man for salvation or cast him to damnation. Luther had for a time the mortal fear of being one of those condemned. And precisely this worry was to him a sign of his condemnation. After all, the teachings of Ockham about man said that he can do something with his inherent strength. He only has to do that which is within him. And he can do a great deal. He can bring himself to complete remorse about his sins, and in that way prepare himself for grace and finally make himself worthy of acceptance. But how is this possible if the experience belies such self-perfection? Luther was under no illusions here. He extracted the last results of the claim of perfect love of God, which he had gotten to know from the works of St. Augustine.

1512
Doctor of Theology Degree Conferred   Plates 47—53

These inner needs of Luther, called his cloister struggle, also continued when he moved again from Erfurt to Wittenberg. This move to Wittenberg was prompted by the continuing arguments among his fellow monks in the Erfurt monastery, which precipitated Luther's journey to Rome. At this time his old friend and fellow monk, John Lang, also went to Wittenberg. Heinrich Boehmer, an important German Luther scholar during the first quarter of our century, believes one may recognize the hidden ways of God in this change of scene, for in this manner, Luther came into more intimate contact with Staupitz. And thereby Wittenberg, and not Erfurt, became the stage for the Reformation. That was important, because Erfurt was in the territory of the archbishop of Magdeburg, where Luther would never have found protection. The elector of Saxony, however, had a certain free hand for various reasons.

So that the professorship of the Old and New Testament of Staupitz could be turned over to Luther, it was necessary for him to earn a doctor's degree. He obtained the degree on Oct. 19, 1512, by participating in a theological debate. The fee, 17 gulden, which had to be paid, was contributed by the elector upon the advice and request of John Staupitz.

And now the so-called "early lectures" of Luther begin: the first lectures on the Psalms (1513—15), the lectures on the Letter of Paul to the Romans (1515—16), on the Letter of Paul to the Galatians (1516), on the Letter to the Hebrews (1517), and the second series of lectures on the Psalms (1519—21) were given.

About this time, at the latest, the event which actually made Luther the Reformer occurred. It is designated as Luther's tower experience, because it took place, according to Luther, in the tower of the "Black Monastery." Luther was given permission to occupy the only heated room in the monastery. That tower no longer exists today. We do not know the exact date when the tower experience took place; we only know its contents: Luther reflected and meditated on chapter 1 of the Letter of Paul to the Romans, verses 16 and 17: "For I am not ashamed of the Gospel; it is the power of God for salvation to everyone who has faith, to the Jew first and also to the Greek. For in it the righteousness of God is revealed through faith; as it is written, 'He who through faith is righteous shall live.'"

It occurred to Luther that the "righteousness of God" which is discussed in this chapter was not to be understood as a characteristic of God, which must set us in terror and fear; but on the contrary, the "righteousness of God" is to be considered as a gift, which God has presented to us contrary to our merit, based on the deliverance through Jesus Christ.

This realization of righteousness as a gift of God is in the final analysis an exegetical knowledge, which comes to a scholar carefully studying the Holy Scripture. But Luther accepted this discovery not only intellectually but rather with every fiber of his being. It became the foundation of his life. Naturally, Luther considered it valid to continue to search for sanctification. But now he took comfort in the realization that forgiveness is assured by the gift of God. He had found the merciful God. The Christian is a sinner in reality, but at the same time, he is righteous by the mercy of God through faith in Jesus Christ. Here we stand before Luther's paradoxical anthropology that man is at the same time righteous and a sinner, *simul iustus, simul peccator*. Naturally, the prerequisites for Luther's enlightenment were in the volumes he had read, e.g., in the works of St. Augustine and the Mystics, which Luther, however, had read in an uncritical manner. Contemporaries had also contributed to the discovery Luther made in the tower. Luther recognized with gratitude that John Staupitz had helped him spiritually. But above all, the Holy Scriptures, in particular the Letters of Paul, were decisive in the "discovery in the tower."

What now followed was basically only the consequences of this rediscovery of the Gospel. It permitted Luther to become first a critic of his church, and because his church did not respond to his criticism, a new confession originated. This course of events distinguishes Luther from all the other reformers before him.

1514

Indulgence Traffic for the Construction
of St. Peter's in Rome
Plates 54—59

In 1514 the pope issued a bull calling for a renewed sale of indulgences to benefit the construction of St. Peter's in Rome. The sale would also aid the archbishop of Mainz, Albert of Hohenzollern. This prince had obtained a high office in the church long before attaining the required minimal age and in addition, now held three ecclesiastical offices, which, according to canon law, was also illegal. Consequently, the archbishop had to secure a special papal dispensation, for which he had to pay a considerable sum of money to the Curia in Rome. Archbishop Albert had borrowed the necessary money from the financially solvent banking house of the Fuggers in Augsburg, who, in order to guarantee the repayment of the loan, had arranged with Pope Leo X for the sale of an indulgence with part of the proceeds going to the archbishop.

A letter of indulgence guaranteed for the purchaser or for someone who had died a reduction of the punishment for sins as well as the time to be spent in purgatory. Besides that, one was able to purchase some relief from the demands of confession and fasting periods. During the time Luther was in Wittenberg, John Tetzel, born in Pirna, near Dresden, and now an unscrupulous Dominican monk from St. Paul's Convent in Leipzig, sold these indulgences. As prescribed, a representative of the Fugger bank traveled with Tetzel, who was a clever salesman. The well-known phrase, "As soon as the coin in the coffer rings, the soul from purgatory springs," was never uttered by Tetzel, but it suits his methods of salesmanship well.

Frederick the Wise forbade the appearance of Tetzel in electoral Saxony. After all, the money raised would benefit the Hohenzollerns, and the elector was not interested in abetting this family's rise to power. In spite of that, devout people from Wittenberg, concerned with the salvation of their souls or that of those who had died, found a way to purchase indulgences, as it was only a 18-mile trip from Wittenberg to Jueterbog.

Luther learned from his parishioners the terrible consequences of the indulgence traffic. In addition he was bombarded from all sides with oral and written questions about indulgences, and he heard how the church and religion had become the objects of mockery. The straw that broke the camel's back was the *Summary Instruction* or *Instructio Summaria* of Albert, a document which the archbishop himself certainly did not write. This brief instructional guide for the salesmen of indulgences stated that the purchase of the indulgence was to be considered as the reconciliating of man with God, e.g., a person was able to purchase it for the benefit of the dead without having himself repented and without making a personal confession.

PLATE 27. At this place Luther is supposed to have said, "Help me, St. Anna, I want to become a monk." The marker indicates that with a bolt of lightning young Luther was shown the road to the Reformation. It is located approximately one-half mile from the village of Stotternheim.

PLATE 28. The rays of the afternoon sun strike one of the portals of the monastery of the Augustinian Order of Hermits in Erfurt.

PLATE 29. Former main gate and guesthouse of the monastery of the Augustinian Order of Hermits in Erfurt. It is one of the last original structures of the monastery standing today. Luther was greeted here in a friendly manner on July 17, 1505.

PLATE 30. Courtyard of the monastery of the Augustinian Order of Hermits in Erfurt. View toward what is known today as Luther's cell—the one with the opened window over the cloister walk. During his twice-interrupted five-year stay at the monastery, Luther was assigned various cells. It is assumed he occupied this one after his return from his journey to Rome in 1511.

PLATE 31. Main portal of the monastery church of the Augustinian Order of Hermits in Erfurt. The church was destroyed during World War II and has been completely rebuilt, as well as other buildings of the monastery, after the air attack on Feb. 25, 1945.

PLATE 32. Interior view of the monastery church of the Augustinian Order of Hermits in Erfurt. View toward the east. In front of the altar is the stone grave marker of Johannes Zachariae, the Augustinian monk from Erfurt who was instrumental in convicting the "completely undefeatable and most highly educated John Huss" in 1415.

PLATE 33. The stone grave marker of Johannes Zachariae in front of the altar of the monastery church in Erfurt. While Luther was taking his monastic vows, as was customary, he lay with his arms outstretched on this grave marker, forming a cross.

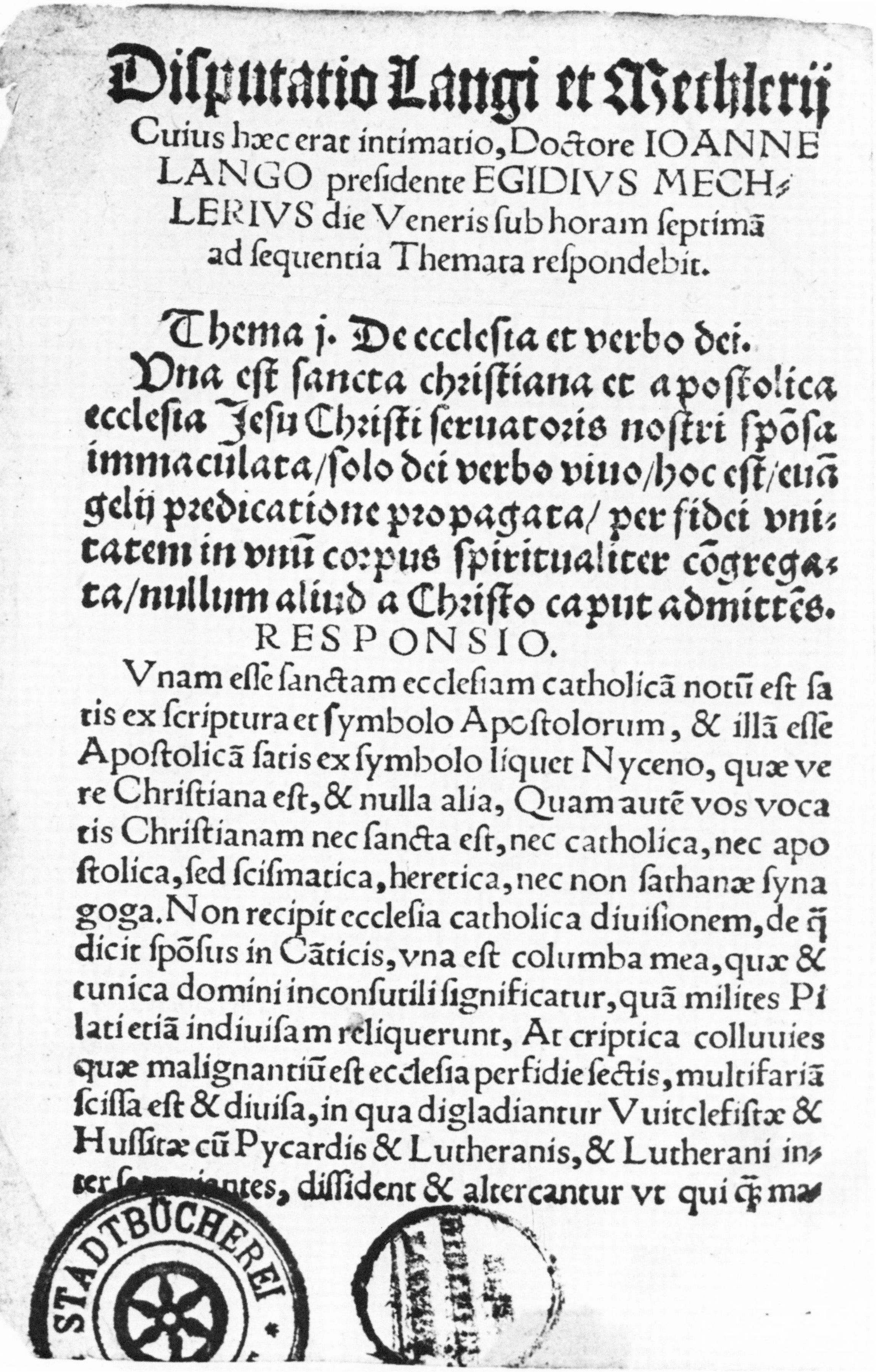

Disputatio Langi et Mechlerij

Cuius hæc erat intimatio, Doctore IOANNE
LANGO presidente EGIDIVS MECH-
LERIVS die Veneris sub horam septimā
ad sequentia Themata respondebit.

Thema j. De ecclesia et verbo dei.

Vna est sancta christiana et apostolica
ecclesia Iesu Christi seruatoris nostri spōsa
immaculata/solo dei verbo viuo/hoc est/euā
gelij predicatione propagata/ per fidei vni-
tatem in vnū corpus spiritualiter cōgrega-
ta/nullum aliud a Christo caput admittēs.

RESPONSIO.

Vnam esse sanctam ecclesiam catholicā notū est sa
tis ex scriptura et symbolo Apostolorum, & illā esse
Apostolicā satis ex symbolo liquet Nyceno, quæ ve
re Christiana est, & nulla alia, Quam autē vos voca
tis Christianam nec sancta est, nec catholica, nec apo
stolica, sed scismatica, heretica, nec non sathanæ syna
goga. Non recipit ecclesia catholica diuisionem, de q̃
dicit spōsus in Cāticis, vna est columba mea, quæ &
tunica domini inconsutili significatur, quā milites Pi
lati etiā indiuisam reliquerunt, At criptica colluuies
quæ malignantiū est ecclesia perfidie sectis, multifariā
scissa est & diuisa, in qua digladiantur Vuitclefistæ &
Hussitæ cū Pycardis & Lutheranis, & Lutherani in-
ter se⟨........⟩antes, dissident & altercantur vt qui q̃ ma-

PLATE 34. Title page of a writing by John Lang, Luther's colleague and friend in the monastery at Erfurt.
(Wissenschaftliche Allgemeinbibliothek, Erfurt)

Johann v. Staupitz († 1524).

PLATE 35. John Staupitz, prior of the Augustinian Order of Hermits. He was also professor of theology at the University of Wittenberg 1502—12. Painting by an unknown artist. (Monastery St. Peter of the Benedictine Order of Monks in Salzburg)

PLATE 36. The elector of Saxony, Frederick the Wise. Bronze grave marker by Peter Vischer the Younger, 1527. The casting is a masterpiece of the early German Renaissance period. The head is an excellent likeness of the electoral prince. (Castle Church, Wittenberg)

PLATE 37. The castle and Castle Church, erected by the elector of Saxony, Frederick the Wise, in Wittenberg, 1509. The outer structure of the Castle Church was completed in 1499 and became the church of the newly founded University of Wittenberg in 1503. The Castle Church tower with its ornate cupola was later reconstructed.

PLATE 38. Polich von Mellerstadt, professor of medicine and first chancellor of the University of Wittenberg. Painting by an unknown artist, 1608. (Lutherhalle, Wittenberg)

PLATE 39. A gate to the former University of Wittenberg, founded by the elector of Saxony, Frederick the Wise, in 1502. This gate by Konrad Pflueger is one of the last remnants of the former university, established in 1502.

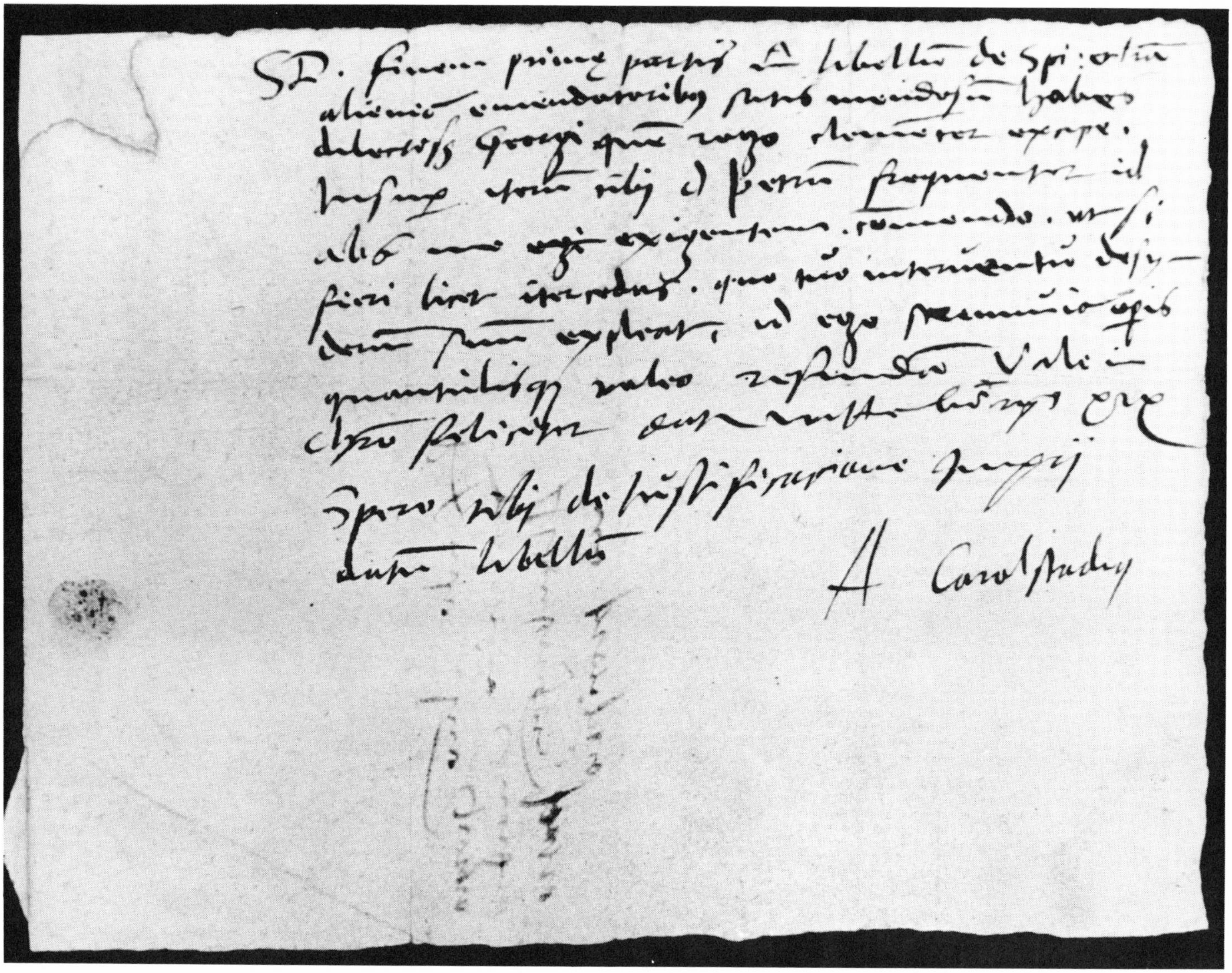

PLATE 40. An original letter by Professor Carlstadt to George Spalatin. It is assumed the letter was written in 1519. (Archiv und Bibliothek, Evangelisches Ministerium, Erfurt)

PLATE 41. Luther's house in Wittenberg, known today as Lutherhalle. It is the former monastery of the Augustinian Order of Hermits, also called "Black Monastery." Luther lived in this building from 1508 until his death in 1546. It was presented to him by Frederick the Wise in 1526. To the right of the tower were the family rooms. Today the building serves as an archive and museum of the Reformation period.

PLATE 42. Lecture podium of the former University of Wittenberg, by an unknown artist, ca. 1600. Above the lectern is a painting of Martin Luther, below are paintings of the first chancellor of the university, Polich von Mellerstadt, and the coat of arms of the four colleges of the former university. (Lutherhalle, Wittenberg)

PLATE 43. An old well in the courtyard of the former "Black Monastery," the monastery of the Augustinian Order Hermits in Wittenberg.

PLATE 44. John Reuchlin, Greek scholar and author of a Hebrew Grammar text. An old woodcut by an unknown artist. (Reuchlinhaus, Stadt Pforzheim)

PLATE 45. Cloister walk of the monastery of the Augustinian Order of Hermits in Erfurt, a familiar path for the young monk, who entered its gates in 1505.

PLATE 46. St. Peter's Square in Rome. The pope is blessing the crowd from the balcony of the partially completed St. Peter's Basilica. Engraving by an unknown artist, second half of the 16th century. From "Speculum Romanae Magnificentiae."

PLATE 47. Market Square in Wittenberg. In the foreground, statues of Luther and Melanchthon erected in the middle of the 19th century. At the left, the City Hall. At the right—not shown—the former apothecary of Lucas Cranach the Elder. In the background, the City Church which Luther later called his own church.

PLATE 48. Dr. Martin Luther as the serious professor and scholar in academic attire with robe and beret. Luther obtained the degree, doctor of theology, on Oct. 19, 1512, from the University of Wittenberg. Painting by Lucas Cranach the Elder, 1528. (Kunstsammlungen zu Weimar)

PLATE 49. Luther Room in the Luther House in Wittenberg. At the left is the beautiful tile stove with illustrations of the Evangelists on the lower section of the stove. Figures representing the liberal arts, among them "Lady Music," are located above them. The room has been preserved with its walls and ceiling covered with painted wooden panels. (Lutherhalle, Wittenberg)

PLATE 50. City Church in Wittenberg. View toward the Altarpiece by Lucas Cranach the Elder. It is considered the artist's last completed work, 1547. The pulpit, which Luther used, is now located in the Lutherhalle.

PLATE 51. Last remnants of Cranach's workshop in Wittenberg. View from the courtyard of the former apothecary of Lucas Cranach at the Market Square. The apothecary is still in operation today.

PLATE 52. Lucas Cranach the Elder at the left. At the right, Martin Luther pointing toward the Word of the Bible. On top of Cranach's head can be seen a portion of the blood which pours in a great arch from the wound in the side of the crucified Savior. Detail from the Altarpiece by Lucas Cranach the Younger, 1555. (City Church, Weimar)

PLATE 53. Altarpiece, City Church, Weimar. Epitaph of Lucas Cranach the Elder, illustrating the artist as the symbol of man, comforted in his struggle with sin and death. On the cross, Jesus Christ, the crucified Son of God. His blood streaming from His side cleansing our sins. At the left, death and the devil are pierced by Christ with the spear of victory. At the right, John the Baptist, Christ's forerunner, points toward Jesus, symbol of God's love, the Lamb of God. At the right, Luther with his finger resting on the Word of the Bible, Hebrews 4:16. Painting by Lucas Cranach the Elder completed by his son Lucas Cranach the Younger, after 1553.

PLATE 54. Man is chased by death and the devil. The painting illustrates the helplessness of man and the dreaded fires of purgatory. Detail from the Altarpiece by Lucas Cranach the Younger, 1555. (City Church, Weimar)

IOHANNES TETZELIUS, LIPSIENSIS

MISNICUS, MONACHUS ORDINIS SANCTI DOMINICI

FRANCOFURTI AD ODERAM, PRÆCO, FORNICARIUS ET

NUNDINATOR, BULLARUM PAPALIUM

INDULGENTIARUM Anno 1517

Denatus d 7 August Anno 1519

PLATE 55. The Dominican monk John Tetzel, as an indulgence salesman. Engraving by J. J. Vogel, 1727. (Lutherhalle, Wittenberg)

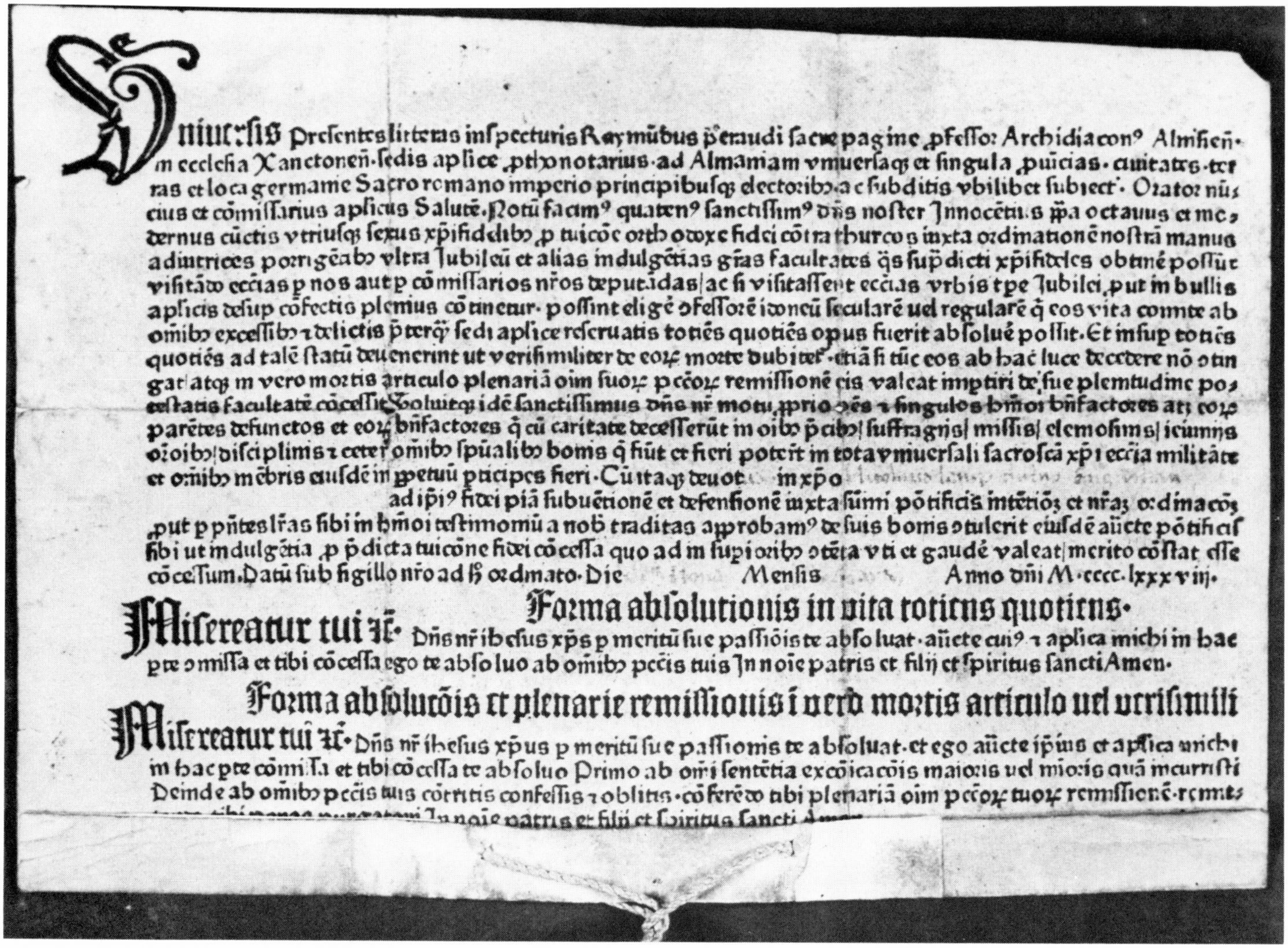

Vniuersis presentes litteras inspecturis Raymundus peraudi sacre pagine professor Archidiaconus Alnisien-
sis in ecclesia Xanctonensi sedis apostolice prothonotarius ad Almaniam vniuersasque et singula prouincias ciuitates ter-
ras et loca germanie Sacro romano imperio principibusque electoribus ac subditis vbilibet subiect. Orator nun-
cius et commissarius apostolicus Salutem. Notum facimus quatenus sanctissimus dominus noster Innocentius papa octauus et mo-
dernus cunctis vtriusque sexus christifidelibus pro tuitione orthodoxe fidei contra thurcos iuxta ordinationem nostram manus
adiutrices porrigentibus vltra Jubileum et alias indulgentias gratias facultates quas supradicti christifideles obtinere possunt
visitando ecclesias per nos aut per commissarios nostros deputandas ac si visitassent ecclesias vrbis tempore Jubilei prout in bullis
apostolicis desuper confectis plenius continetur. possint eligere confessorem idoneum secularem vel regularem qui eos vita comite ab
omnibus excessibus et delictis preterquam sedi apostolice reseruatis toties quoties opus fuerit absoluere possit. Et insuper toties
quoties ad talem statum deuenerint ut verisimiliter de eorum morte dubitetur. etiam si tunc eos ab hac luce decedere non contin-
gat atque in vero mortis articulo plenariam omnium suorum peccatorum remissionem eis valeat impartiri de sue plenitudine po-
testatis facultatem concessit. Voluitque idem sanctissimus dominus noster motu proprio omnes et singulos huiusmodi benefactores atque eorum
parentes defunctos et eorum benefactores qui cum caritate decesserunt in omnibus precibus suffragiis missis elemosinis ieiuniis
orationibus disciplinis et ceteris omnibus spiritualibus bonis que fiunt et fieri poterunt in tota vniuersali sacrosancta christi ecclesia militante
et omnibus membris eiusdem in perpetuum participes fieri. Cum itaque deuot in christo
ad ipsius fidei piam subuentionem et defensionem iuxta summi pontificis intentionem et nostram ordinationem
prout per presentes litteras sibi in huiusmodi testimonium a nobis traditas approbamus de suis bonis contulerit eiusdem auctoritate pontificis
sibi ut indulgentia prout predicta tuitione fidei concessa quo ad in superioribus contenta vti et gaudere valeat merito constat esse
concessum. Datum sub sigillo nostro ad hoc ordinato. Die Mensis Anno domini M.cccc.lxxxviij.

Forma absolutionis in vita toticus quoticus.

Misereatur tui etc. Dominus noster ihesus christus per meritum sue passionis te absoluat. auctoritate cuius et apostolica michi in hac
parte commissa et tibi concessa ego te absoluo ab omnibus peccatis tuis In nomine patris et filij et spiritus sancti Amen.

Forma absolutionis et plenarie remissionis in vero mortis articulo vel verisimili

Misereatur tui etc. Dominus noster ihesus christus per meritum sue passionis te absoluat. et ego auctoritate ipsius et apostolica michi
in hac parte commissa et tibi concessa te absoluo Primo ab omni sententia excommunicationis maioris vel minoris quam incurristi
Deinde ab omnibus peccatis tuis contritis confessis et oblitis. conferendo tibi plenariam omnium peccatorum tuorum remissionem remit-
tendo tibi penas purgatorij In nomine patris et filij et spiritus sancti Amen.

PLATE 56. An original letter of indulgence, dated 1488. (Archiv und Bibliothek, Evangelisches Ministerium, Erfurt)

LEO · X · PAPA · FLORENTIN:

PLATE 57. Pope Leo X, who decreed the sale of indulgences for the construction of St. Peter's in Rome. Woodcut by an unknown artist, 16th century. (Lutherhalle, Wittenberg)

IACOBVS·FVGGER·CIVIS·AVGVSTÆ

PLATE 58. Jacob Fugger of the banking house in Augsburg. Woodcut by Hans Burgkmair, 1510—12. (Lutherhalle, Wittenberg)

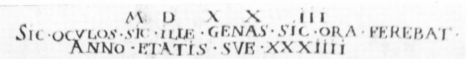

PLATE 59. Cardinal Albert of Brandenburg, archbishop of Magdeburg, archbishop and administrator of Halberstadt, and electoral prince of Mainz. Engraving by Albrecht Duerer, 1519. (Lutherhalle, Wittenberg)

III. The Birth of Lutheranism and Years of Storm, 1517–1525

1517

Posting the 95 Theses   **Plates 60—61**

Luther, the serious Christian, who had discovered that he owed his salvation to deliverance through Jesus Christ, thought he must proclaim this message, and as a teacher and doctor of theology, he felt even more keenly that this was his responsibility. Therefore he wanted to apply a certain amount of pressure on the archbishop of Mainz in the form of a public act. According to Luther, the archbishop had only given his name to that terrible manuscript, the *Instructio Summaria,* because of his youthful immaturity and lack of theological knowledge. Therefore he invited the members of the university to a public debate about the beneficial power of indulgences.

Catholic scholars have recently questioned whether the 95 Theses printed in Latin were actually posted on the door of the Castle Church on Oct. 31, 1517, on the eve of this church's great festival, the Feast of All Saints. The actual posting of the Theses cannot be proven; nevertheless, the date remains very probable. There was no great public demonstration when Luther posted his Theses, for the majority of the people were not familiar with the Latin language. Frequently, the Castle Church door was used as a bulletin board by the students and the faculty of the university.

At the same time, Luther sent an additional copy of the Theses to the advisers of the archbishop to bring this topic to his attention. Besides adding a short treatise on indulgences, Luther enclosed a letter in which he demanded that the archbishop withdraw the *Instructio Summaria*. Similar documents were also sent to Bishop Jerome Schulze of Brandenburg.

In no way did Luther act improperly, since there was not as yet officially a dogma on indulgences at that time. It was not formulated until the Council of Trent. Besides that, the 95 Theses did not even contain a general attack on the concept of indulgence. Luther attacked only the rise of indulgences as a substitute for repentance. He expressed the nucleus of his belief in the 62nd thesis, which differed from the general practice of the church: "The true treasure of the church is the most holy Gospel of the glory and grace of God" (*Luther's Works,* Vol. 31 [Philadelphia: Muhlenberg Press, 1957], p. 31).

1518

The Conference in Heidelberg   **Plate 62**

At first the 95 Theses created no response and no one even came for the debate. Also Luther received no answer from his superiors. Then he sent copies of his Theses to some of his friends, and now they were copied by hand and reproduced by the printer, and they were translated, thus becoming in a short time well known throughout Germany.

With the widespread distribution of the 95 Theses the great debate began. All kinds of documents appeared. There were those who sided with Luther and those who were opposed. Before long the dispute reached Rome, at first coming into the hands of the highest official of Luther's order. Luther was given an opportunity to speak, when Staupitz, as a special gesture of friendliness, assigned him to deliver the Theses and chair the discussion in the debate at the General Chapter meeting of the Augustinian Order of Hermits at Heidelberg in April 1518. These Theses show us the essentials of the development of Luther's theology. He designates true theology as the theology of the cross, the *theologia crucis*. Here in Heidelberg Luther also dismissed the philosophy of William

Ockham and the metaphysics of Aristotle, thereby attracting many a young Humanist.

1518

With Cardinal Cajetan in Augsburg   Plates 63—68

The situation became dangerous for Luther when the Dominicans[7] intensified their denunciations in Rome. An overheard discussion played a role here in which Luther had been involved after a sermon he delivered before the nobility of the court of Dresden.[8] Duke George had not been in residence at that time.

A final attempt to quench the flames was sanctioned by the pope. He instructed the temporary papal legate in Germany, Cardinal Cajetan, to interrogate Luther carefully in Augsburg, but to avoid any sort of argument. Luther was indebted to his sovereign, Elector Frederick the Wise, for this kindness, for he wanted to protect the successful professor of his newly founded university, and the pope did not want to offend the elector on account of the impending election of the king.[9] Presumably, George Spalatin, the private secretary of the Court of Saxony and spiritual adviser to Frederick the Wise, had interceded in behalf of Luther, who never actually met the elector.

Although Cajetan was conscious of his responsibility[10] and had a superior knowledge of theology, he was unable to persuade Luther in three separate meetings to recant as demanded by Rome. It was a stalemate, and under the cover of darkness Luther left the city. In the meantime Staupitz had relieved Luther of all duties to the order so that he had the freedom to devote his full attention to these matters.

Luther's several negotiations with the pope's chamberlain, Charles von Miltitz, accomplished even less. Miltitz had taken it upon himself to go beyond the task assigned to him by Rome in making unauthorized promises to Luther.

1519

Leipzig Debate Plates 69—72

Dr. John Eck, professor of theology at Ingolstadt, succeeded in luring Luther into a public debate, which took place in Leipzig in July, 1519. In this debate Eck was successful in forcing Luther to admit that among the articles of the Hussites many were genuinely Christian and evangelical. This statement caused the duke of Saxony, George, later called The Bearded, to become Luther's bitter enemy, since the duke's mother had been the daughter of a converted Hussite.

1518

Melanchthon's Arrival in Wittenberg Plates 73—76

In the meantime, there was an important development in Wittenberg. In 1518 the university succeeded in obtaining as professor of Greek the 21-year-old Philipp Melanchthon, who was the grandnephew of the famous Humanist John Reuchlin. Melanchthon was small of physical stature but of great intellect. Soon Luther sat at his feet to improve his knowledge of Greek. A close friendship developed quickly between the two modern and towering men. Melanchthon, born Philipp Schwartzerd from Bretten, located in the hills of the Neckar River, had accompanied Luther to the debate in Leipzig. As anxious as the diplomatic scholar could be, nevertheless Melanchthon did not retreat from Luther's side when on June 15, 1520, the *Exsurge, Domine,* the bull threatening papal ban against Luther, was issued and the Reformer burned it in front of the Elster Gate in Wittenberg on Dec. 10, 1520, together with a copy of the canon law and other books of the church. Melanchthon presented the forthcoming Lutheran Church with its first dogmatic writing, the *Loci communes rerum theologicarum* (1521), unequaled in its clarity and polished formulation.

1521

The Edict of Worms Plates 77—82

During this time of utmost external afflictions, Luther's first great tracts of the Reformation originated: *To the Christian Nobility of the German Nation Concerning the Reform of the Christian Estate, The Freedom of a Christian,* and *The Babylonian Captivity of the Church,* as well as numerous other religious tracts.

After many negotiations, Frederick the Wise succeeded in bringing Luther to a hearing before the emperor and the diet held at Worms.

Luther did not permit himself to be detained from this journey, either by illness or by a trick of his opponents to lure him to the Ebernburg Castle of Franz von Sickingen. The detour would have caused a delay, and Luther would not have arrived in Worms at the appointed time. Frederick the Wise, who was concerned for Luther, dispatched a warning at the last moment through Spalatin. Luther replied, "If there were as many devils in Worms as tiles on the rooftops, nevertheless, I want to go there."

Thus Luther, the 36-year-old theologian, stood before the German princes in Worms on April 17 and 18, 1521. Before him sat the 21-year-old king, Charles V, on whose realm the sun did not set. Luther refused to recant his writings. The last few words of his speech before the diet have become famous: "Therefore, I can and will recant nothing, because it is neither safe nor right to act against conscience. God help me. Amen!"

The following day Charles V announced his decision to set his "kingdoms, territories, friends, body and blood, life and soul" against the single erring brother, who, according to the king, "stood against the belief of all Christendom."

The papal ban, already issued on Jan. 3, 1521, was followed by the imperial ban, which declared Luther as *vogelfrei,* a wanted man, who could be killed on sight. The ban also threatened anyone who "harbored him, or gave him food or drink." In addition, all of Luther's books were to be burned and all books printed in Germany had to be censored by the

90

officials of the church. That was the Edict of Worms, and the rulers of each territory had to abide by it and carry it out.

Frederick had anticipated these actions. Therefore, an attack on Luther was staged near Altenstein, and the Reformer was brought in a form of protective custody to the nearby Wartburg Castle. Soon "Junker Joerg," as Luther was called, grew a beard and let his hair grow in order to change his appearance from that of a monk to that of a knight. Lucas Cranach, to whom we are indebted for many portraits of the Reformation period, made a likeness of Luther in December 1521 when he once secretly came to Wittenberg during Luther's stay at the Wartburg.

1521

Safe at the Wartburg Castle   Plates 83—89

Luther worked with intensity during his 10-month forced loneliness and stillness at the Wartburg Castle.

His most famous work was the German translation of the New Testament from the Greek text which Desiderus Erasmus had published just a few years earlier. To be sure, Luther and Melanchthon looked over the translation before it went into print following Luther's return to Wittenberg in 1522. However, Luther's extraordinary grasp of the language, his original, poetical, and expressive use of words makes the translation of the New Testament Luther's own work. For the first time, New High German was utilized in a literary manner. The book was published in September 1522 and thus received the name "Septembertestament." Lucas Cranach and his workshop supplied the woodcuts used in the Book of Revelation. In certain details they are reminiscent of Duerer's work in Nuernberg.

Luther completed at the Wartburg Castle one of his most comforting religious tracts, his exposition of The Magnificat.

He also wrote a controversial treatise *The Judgment of Martin Luther on*

Monastic Vows (De votis monasticis Martini Lutheri iudicium), a tract concerned with the abolition of the monastic system.

He dedicated a small book about confession to Franz von Sickingen, who had offered Luther a sanctuary and protection at the Ebernburg Castle in 1520.

Only a few people knew where Luther was located. Some even mourned his death. It was now evident that Charles V had erred when he thought that it was only a matter of a "single brother." The reform movement continued to move forward, but at first not in the manner that Luther had intended.

1522

Luther's Return to Wittenberg   Plates 90—91

In Wittenberg itself the radicals gained ground. Here priests and monks married. The first was Bartholomaeus Bernhardi, senior pastor in Kemberg, near Wittenberg. Some began to celebrate the Lord's Supper in two forms, that is, they also gave the cup to the laity. This was a custom which had not been practiced for centuries and which only the dissidents, such as the Hussites, had introduced again 100 years previously.

Finally, the abolition of the monastic life was publicly demanded. There were even some minor iconoclastic riots[11] in Wittenberg. Luther's colleague Carlstadt placed himself on the side of the agitators.

Against the will of the elector, Luther left his refuge in the Wartburg Castle, responding to the call of the City Council of Wittenberg, and returned to the city on March 9, 1522. He preached daily for a week in his habit and tonsure. These are the famous *Invocavit Sermons*. (His eight sermons appeared in summary in April 1522 under the title *Receiving Both Kinds in the Sacrament.*) Luther restored peace and order to Wittenberg again, even though he was not able to win back the support of the radical, Carlstadt. Certain earlier abuses were removed. Monks and nuns continued to marry, and in the following year the number of those who left the monastic life grew steadily, even far beyond the limits of Wittenberg.

The evangelical message was also spread by word of mouth and in written form far beyond Wittenberg. Merchants took the writings of the reformers into the farthest corners of Europe, and from the most distant regions young men came to Wittenberg as students in order to hear the new teachings, which they then made known in their homeland.

Amore et studio elucidande veritatis: hec subscripta disputabuntur Wittenberge. Presidente R. P. Martino Luther: Artiu et S. Theologie Magistro: eiusdemq ibidem lectore Ordinario. Quare petit: vt qui non possunt verbis presentes nobiscu disceptare: agant id literis absentes. In noie dni nostri hiesu chri. Ame.

M.D.xvij.

PLATE 60. Printed copy of Luther's 95 Theses in Latin. (Lutherhalle, Wittenberg)

PLATE 61. The door of the Castle Church in Wittenberg that contains the 95 Theses embossed in bronze. The original door burned and was replaced by this metal one, dedicated in 1858.

PLATE 62. City of Heidelberg on the Neckar River. View from the Philosopher's Path toward the castle, where presumably the conference of the Augustinian Order of Hermits took place in 1518.

PLATE 63. Stone relief depicting Pope Paul II at the left and Emperor Charles V at the right. Below, a monk, presumably Martin Luther. Artist unknown, 1535. (Katharinenstrasse 9, Leipzig)

PLATE 64. The duke of Saxony, George the Bearded, who became one of Luther's most bitter enemies. Painting by Lucas Cranach the Elder, between 1534 and 1539. (Wartburg-Stiftung, Eisenach)

PLATE 65. Cloister walk of the monastery of the Carmelites in Augsburg. Luther stayed in this monastery while attending the sessions with the temporary papal legate in Germany, Cardinal Cajetan, in 1518.

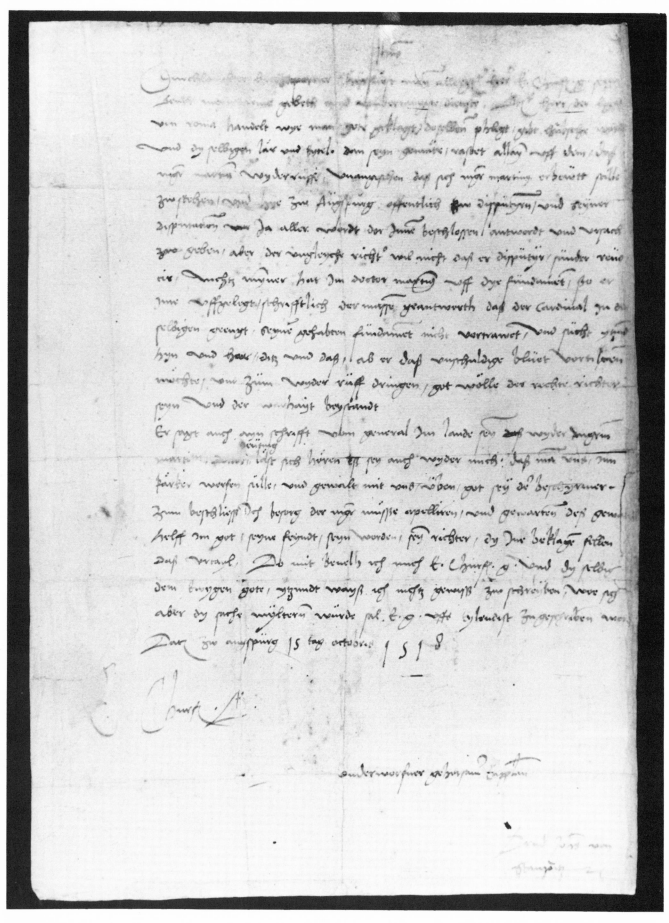

PLATE 66. An original letter by John Staupitz to the elector of Saxony, Frederick the Wise, in which Staupitz reports on Luther's conference with Cardinal Cajetan in Augsburg, 1518. The letter is dated Oct. 15, 1518. (Archiv und Bibliothek, Erfurt)

·EFFIGIES· G· SPALATINI·
·M·D·XXXVII·

PLATE 67. George Burkhardt also called Spalatin, the private secretary of the Court of Saxony and spiritual adviser to Frederick the Wise. Spalatin interceded in behalf of Luther. Painting by Lucas Cranach the Elder, 1537. (Staatliche Kunsthalle, Karlsruhe)

PLATE 68. City of Altenburg. Site of the negotiations between Luther and the pope's private chamberlain, Charles von Miltitz. View toward the castle and the Castle Church.

VERA IMAGO IOHANNIS ECCII
THEOLOGIÆ D. ÆTATIS
SVÆ XLIII

ECK EIN GROSSER FEIND CHRISTI WAR
HAT SEHR VERFOLGT DIE CHRISTLICH SCHAR
MIT SCHREIBEN VND VNNVCZEM GSCHWECZ
BRACHT ER DIE EINFELTIGEN INS NECZ
EIFRIG VND BÖS WAR ALL SEIN SIINN
VERGEBS IM GOT ER IST LANG HIINN.

PLATE 69. Dr. John Eck, professor of theology at the University of Ingolstadt. He debated with Luther in Leipzig in 1519 and forced Luther to admit that the Roman Church may have erred when it convicted John Huss in 1415. Engraving by an unknown artist, 1735. (Lutherhalle, Wittenberg)

PLATE 70. Main portal of the newly reconstructed St. Thomas Church in Leipzig. It was damaged during an air attack on April 12, 1943, and the renovation was completed in 1964.

PLATE 71. St. Thomas Church in Leipzig. Present-day view from the east. The ceremonies for the famous religious debate between Eck and Luther began here in 1519. George Rhau, then the choir master of the now famous *Thomanerchor*, composed a special mass for the occasion.

PLATE 72. The Pleissenburg, in which the religious debate between Luther and Eck took place in July, 1519. Detail of a water color by Gottfried Bachmann, 1782. (Museum fuer Geschichte der Stadt, Leipzig)

1526.
VIVENTIS·POTVIT·DVRERIVS·ORA·PHILIPPI
MENTEM·NON·POTVIT·PINGERE·DOCTA
MANVS
AD

PLATE 73. Philipp Melanchthon, professor of Greek and grandnephew of the famous Humanist, John Reuchlin. Engraving by Albrecht Duerer, 1526. (Lutherhalle, Wittenberg)

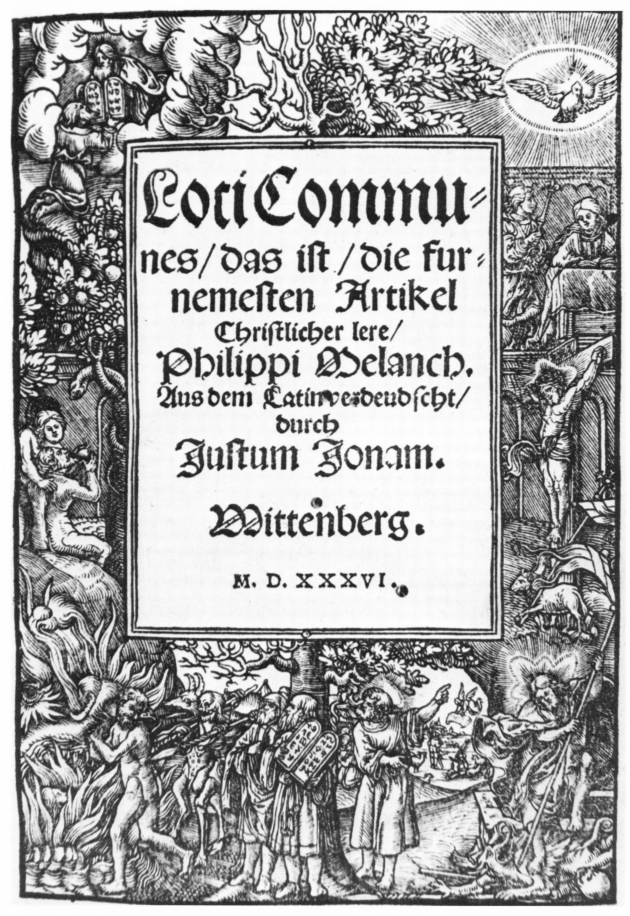

Loci Commu-
nes / das ist / die fur-
nemeſten Artikel
Chriſtlicher lere /
Philippi Melanch.
Aus dem Latin verdeudſcht /
durch
Juſtum Jonam.

Wittenberg.

M. D. XXXVI.

PLATE 74. Title page of Melanchthon's dogmatic work *Loci communes*, Wittenberg, 1536. Translated into German by Justus Jonas. (Evangelisches Pfarramt St. Andreas-Nicolai, Eisleben)

PLATE 75. Melanchthon House in Wittenberg. View from the street. The elector of Saxony, John Frederick, remodeled the house at his own expense in 1535 and a garden was presented to Melanchthon. The back gate of the garden was only 200 feet from the Luther House. The two Reformers spent many pleasant hours in the garden. The second floor contained the family rooms. The building has been well preserved and was partially restored in 1897.

PLATE 76. Melanchthon's Study. The furniture is of later origin. Melanchthon died in this room, surrounded by many of his colleagues and students, on April 19, 1560, at the age of 63. (Melanchthon House, Wittenberg)

PLATE 77. Luther preaching the Gospel from the stone pulpit of the Castle Church in Torgau. Detail from the *Predella* of the Altarpiece by Lucas Cranach the Elder, 1547. (City Church, Wittenberg)

PLATE 78. Title page of the papal bull threatening the ban against Luther, issued in Rome, 1520. (Lutherhalle, Wittenberg)

PLATE 79. City of Worms. The building in which Luther stood before the emperor and the princes at the Diet of Worms in 1521 no longer stands. In the foreground are its last remnants. The cathedral is located in the background.

Vonn der freyheyt
eynß Christenn
menschen.

D. Martinus Luther.

(p. 2172.1.)

Wittembergk·
1521.

PLATE 80. Title page of Luther's Protestant tract *The Freedom of a Christian*, Wittenberg, 1521. (Lutherhalle, Wittenberg)

PLATE 81. Emperor Charles V as a young man. When the emperor sat before Luther on April 17, 1521, Charles V, on whose realm the sun did not set, was only 21 years old. Woodcut by Albrecht Duerer. (Lutherhalle, Wittenberg)

hier wurde
Dr. Martin Luther
am 4 Mai 1521
auf Befehl
Friedrich d Weisen
Kurfürsten von Sachsen
aufgehoben
und nach Schloß Wartburg
geführt.

Er wird trinken vom Bache
am Wege, darum wird er
das Haupt emporheben.
Psalm 110

PLATE 82. Sandstone monument near Altenstein, where the "attack" on Luther took place on May 4, 1521. He was taken from here to the nearby Wartburg Castle in Eisenach.

PLATE 83. The Wartburg Castle after reconstruction in 1965. View from the northeast.

PLATE 84. Luther as Junker Joerg. Painting by Lucas Cranach the Elder, 1522. (Kunstsammlungen zu Weimar)

Deutsch Außlegüg des sieben vñ sechtzigsté Psalmé. võ dem Ostertag. Hymelfart vnd Pfingsten. D. Martinus L.

1521.

Auß der Wartburg geschrieben

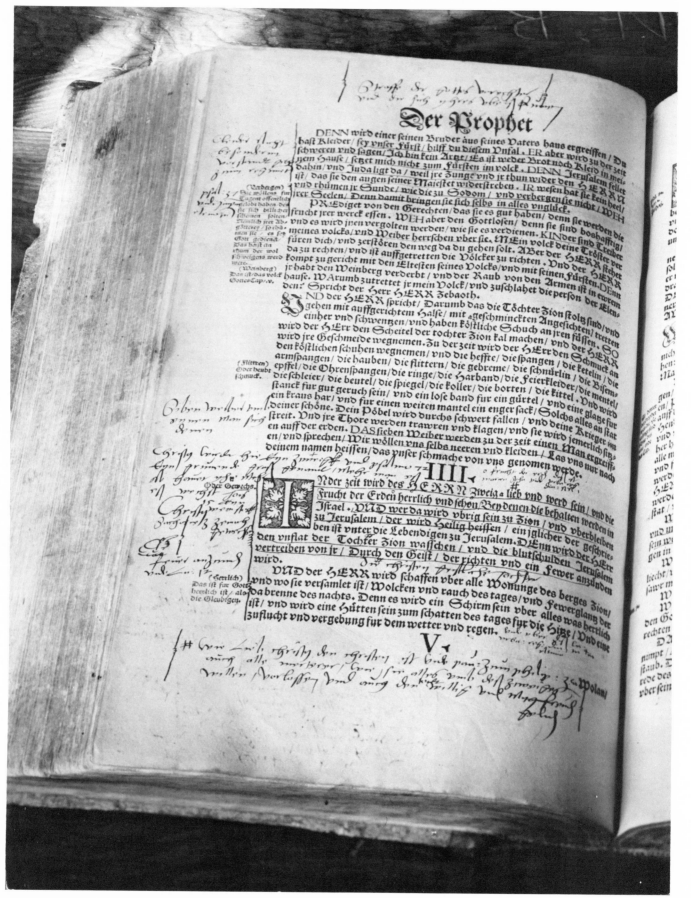

PLATE 87. Luther's room in the Wartburg Castle. The Bible containing Luther's remarks lies on the desk. On the wall are paintings of Luther's parents by Lucas Cranach the Elder and an engraving by the artist depicting Luther as Junker Joerg. The room has been preserved in its original condition.

PLATE 88. Luther's translation of the New Testament, the so-called Septembertestament, which he translated at the Wartburg Castle. Wittenberg, 1522. (Evangelisches Pfarramt St. Andreas-Nicolai, Eisleben)

PLATE 89. The four riders of the Apocalypse. From the Septembertestament, Wittenberg, 1522. Woodcut by Cranach's workshop, 1522. (Evangelisches Pfarramt St. Andreas-Nicolai, Eisleben)

PLATE 90. Bartholomaeus Bernhardi, senior pastor in Kemberg, near Wittenberg. He was the first priest to get married. Detail from the Reformation Altarpiece by Lucas Cranach the Younger, 1565. (Village church in Mildensee, near Dessau)

D. ANDREAS BODENSTEIN. sonst CARLSTADT, auch Nachbar Anders genant.

PLATE 91. Andreas Bodenstein, also called Carlstadt, an iconoclast. An old engraving by an unknown artist. (Lutherhalle, Wittenberg)

IV. Theological Controversies and Religious War, 1525–1555

1525

The Peasants' War

Plates 92—98

The "Wittenberg Movement" had shown what can happen when the dam breaks, and even more was to follow. Dissatisfaction had fermented for a long time among the peasants, the segment of the populace which had been the most neglected economically and socially. The peasants had heard a great deal from the theologians about "the freedom of a Christian." What could be more appropriate from them than to seize such words! In doing this, they did not understand the religious meaning of these words. (Luther meant an inner freedom of the reborn man.) On the contrary, the peasants gave the words a social significance (freedom from the economic bondage in feudalism).

A former preacher from Zwickau, Thomas Muenzer, who in the beginning was a follower of Luther, came to Muehlhausen, after residing in several other locations, and preached more and more passionately a new road to salvation. [12] He saw this road in the experience of the cross. Beyond that, believing to be chosen, he was not aware of realities. He reinforced the protesting peasants in central Germany and contributed to their catastrophe at Frankenhausen on May 15, 1525. He himself was sacrificed to its cause.

Luther is often criticized for his stand in the Peasants' War. First he had appealed to the princes and rulers in his tract *Admonition to Peace: A Reply to the Twelve Articles of the Peasants in Swabia* and asked them fervently to react with humility and penitence to the judgment of God, namely, the peasant rebellion. He had accepted in part the demands of the peasants. However, he rejected revolution as a method. Above all, he opposed the right of the peasants to establish their demands on the basis of the Gospel.

His second writing, which was composed after the outbreak of the actual revolt, bears the title: *Against the Robbing and Murdering Hordes of Peasants.* The content of this tract matches the harsh title. Luther demanded that the princes destroy the revolutionaries. It is difficult for us to justify this second tract dealing with the peasants' revolt, even if we take into consideration Luther's anguish about the forceful overthrow of the social order, as well as his fear of a falsification of the teaching of the Gospel, and beyond that, reflect upon the proclaimed judgment in his third tract, *An Open Letter Concerning the Hard Book Against the Peasants,* in which he admonishes the raging tyrants, who are not saturated with the thirst of blood even after the battle is over.

The year of the Peasants' War brought for Luther two important personal events. Even before the battle of Frankenhausen, his protector, Frederick the Wise, died. His brother, John the Steadfast, succeeded him and ruled until 1532, when John's son, John Frederick the Magnanimous, followed him into that office. Both princes stood openly and firmly on the side of the Reformation. The other important event was Luther's marriage.

1525

Luther's Marriage   Plates 99—102

On June 13, 1525, soon after the battle of Frankenhausen, Luther was married to the former nun Katharine von Bora. Since her escape from the Convent Nimbschen near Grimma on the Saturday before Easter, April 7, 1523, she had lived in Wittenberg. Luther considered marriage as a creation of God, but he emphasized throughout his lifetime that a life without marriage is considerably more comfortable. Luther, however, thought that what he preached to others he ought to practice himself. Furthermore, Luther's aged father was hoping for a grandson. Finally, Luther wished to show through his marriage his faith in God during these difficult times. Perhaps he didn't expect that such a beautiful union would result from such a hasty step, as one can detect from his letters and other statements. The couple did have six children.

1525

The Bondage of the Will   Plate 103

From this time dates *The Bondage of the Will (De servo arbitrio).* [13] In this work, which Luther considers one of his greatest, the Reformer argues against a writing by the Humanist Erasmus of Rotterdam, *The Freedom of the Will (De libero arbitrio),* published in 1524.

1526

Luther the Reformer   Plates 104—108

Now we are confronted with the familiar figure of Luther the Reformer. He was the professor who prepared and held his lectures energetically and enthusiastically and carried out his academic duties to the fullest and who, just as diligently, served his parish with sermons and pastoral work. He also directly or indirectly guided the progress of the Reformation from Wittenberg; first in the electorate, then across Germany, and ultimately throughout all of Europe. Aside from that he also performed his pastoral duties to individuals near and far. In his letters, which fill many volumes today, he answered many personal questions.

He was already giving the publishers of his time plenty to do. His wife complained that he never took royalties from them and that he alone made the publishers wealthy. It was his opinion that he had to pass on the joyful tidings of the Gospel freely since he himself had received the tidings free of charge.

He suffered from several illnesses and attacks of exhaustion, but above all, he suffered from charges and defamations by his opponents. Luther suffered, too, when other people were harmed, e.g., the citizens of Leipzig who on account of their confession to the evangelical belief had been driven out of their homeland by Duke George.

We also remember Luther as a conversationalist. He often sat at the table with his circle of friends, colleagues, and boarders giving his time to talk—sometimes serious, sometimes humorous. And he closes one eye as one or the other student was seen taking notes. These notes have been preserved, so that today we can know what the topic of conversation was. There were important theological and political discussions, but also things to which the man of the 20th-century would shake his head. Luther was no saint, and he was also not infallible. When Luther was informed about an astronomer (they had Nicolas Copernicus in mind) who said the earth moved around the sun, Luther could only retort with the quotation in Joshua 10:12, wherein Joshua commanded the sun—not the earth—to stand still (in Gibeon). [14]

They also often made music in this circle of friends. Luther loved music. Through his musical talent he was in a position to present the Christian community the first evangelical songs and the first small hymnal.

1529

Luther and Zwingli at Marburg   Plates 109—112

As the Reformation movement progressed, it became evident that Luther was not the only opponent who successfully confronted the church of Rome. Ulrich Zwingli had at first challenged the political abuses in Zurich. He protested against those adventurous, young Swiss who served in the armies of foreign powers as mercenaries. In 1522 Zwingli began to attack ecclesiastical institutions, e.g., the laws concerning fasting. Finally, he had demanded the freedom "to preach the Gospel" and the right of priests to marry. In spite of all this, his movement did not coincide with that of Luther.

The big difference between Zwingli and Luther concerned the question of the Lord's Supper. Luther already had a disagreement with Carlstadt about this problem. Carlstadt's opinion has remained unimportant in the course of time. Zwingli understood the Lord's Supper to be *Gedaechtnismahl,* purely a memorial feast. The bread and the wine only "signify" Christ's body and blood. Zwingli's understanding of the Sacrament is based upon a literal interpretation of Christ's "ascent into the sky to the heavens." Christ now "sits at the right hand of God" outside of our earthly sphere. Therefore, He cannot be present bodily in the Lord's Supper.

Luther refuted this by saying that after Christ ascended into heaven He cannot be localized in space just as God cannot be. In this Luther deviates from the medieval view of the world. The risen Christ is always everywhere *ubique.* Therefore He can be present everywhere in the bread and the wine at the same time. This is Luther's concept of *ubiquity.*

Out of this controversy came Luther's great *Confession Concerning Christ's Supper* in 1528.

This difference of opinion on the Lord's Supper prevented the collaboration of the two reformers. Zwingli, who was very politically oriented, sensed this much more fervently than Luther. Also the young duke, Philip of Hesse, who had placed himself on the side of the evangelical movement since the middle of the 1520s, wished a union of all evangelicals into a political alliance. Therefore he invited the Wittenberg theologians and Zwingli, together with other theologians who leaned towards Zwingli's theology, to a religious discussion at his residence at the Marburg Castle in 1529. They did agree on fourteen of the fifteen articles. However, Luther felt compelled to say, in addition to the controversy dealing with the Lord's Supper, that the opposition had a "different spirit." Thus the die was cast that there would be more than one reform movement.

This divisiveness showed itself only too clearly at the Diet of Augsburg, which took place the following year with Charles V in attendance. He had in the meantime become emperor of the Holy Roman Empire and had returned to Germany for the first time after nine years, having been previously detained by wars. More decisiveness was to be expected from this diet than from the preceding ones.

1529

Speyer "Protestants" Plate 113

At the first Diet of Speyer, as well as at the second, the religious questions had been left in abeyance. In 1526 the evangelicals had very bravely appeared, and it had only been stipulated with respect to the Edict of Worms that each prince and dignitary of the imperial diet should act in such a manner "that they might hope and trust to be found responsible in the service of God and His Imperial Majesty." Even at the diet in 1529 the evangelical princes had ceremoniously entered a protest when the Catholic party tried to advance more energetically. This act was recorded in the minutes and gave the evangelicals the name "Protestants." Since then, the evangelical and Catholic states in the empire have been separated according to constitutional law.

1530

Confessio Augustana Plates 114—117

At the Diet of Augsburg in 1530 the Wittenberg theologians and councilors of the elector presented the Augsburg Confession (*Confessio Augustana*), which essentially was drafted by Philipp Melanchthon. They had to travel to southern Germany without Luther, for he was under the imperial ban and therefore remained at the Coburg Castle, the last place of refuge on their journey to Augsburg before entering the land of the

131

opposition. At the Coburg Castle Luther was still under the protection of the elector of Saxony.

Zwingli brought a separate confession to the diet.

In addition, four southern German cities, among them Strasbourg, submitted their own confession.

Thus the disunity of the evangelicals became quite obvious to everyone at the diet.

Emperor Charles V thought he could dismiss the *Confessio Augustana* by the written confutation of a few Catholic theologians, among them John Eck.

The Augsburg Confession is truly a sound evangelical document. Since, however, the evangelicals wanted above all to show that they were in essential agreement with the Catholic believers, Melanchthon intentionally did not touch a few hot irons. Statements in the Augsburg Confession are lacking on the papacy, purgatory, indulgences, and the Catholic concept of the Lord's Supper. When Luther was asked for his approval of the document, he left it unchanged because he felt "almost good" about it, even if he stated that he "would not have been able to walk so softly and gently." The *Confessio Augustana* became the abiding document of the Lutheran faith.

1531

The Schmalkaldic League   Plate 118

At the Diet of Augsburg in 1530 no definite decision was reached. The evangelicals rightfully feared an armed conflict with the emperor as soon as he had his hands free from matters dealing with foreign policy. Therefore the evangelicals prepared themselves and concluded a defensive alliance in Schmalkalden in 1531. At first this alliance was to last six years. Luther now also agreed to an eventual military stand against the emperor. In the meantime the lawyers had found justification for it in a political analysis of the situation. In their opinion the territorial princes formed the

God-given ruling body. The emperor was considered to be only the elected official of the territorial princes, who were actually responsible for the spiritual welfare of their subjects.

1534

First Complete German Bible   **Plates 119—120**

During these uncertain times and after much effort, the German translation of the entire Bible was published. In collaboration with a group of colleagues and experts, Luther had completed the giant work and with it presented the German people his most important book and through it gave them a language for centuries to come.

1537

Schmalkaldic Articles   **Plate 121**

The confessional writing which expresses most purely and clearly the evangelical faith appeared in 1537. Luther prepared this work, the Schmalkaldic Articles, for a promised general church council. The articles contain the doctrine which the evangelicals were to defend.

1541

Religious Debate in Regensburg   **Plate 122**

Meanwhile, the emperor was severely plagued with problems in foreign politics. The Turks, in 1529, had abandoned their position before the gates of Vienna but nevertheless gave Charles V his greatest worry. Therefore he had to put off the religious questions in Germany. The opposing parties attempted once again to come to an agreement by means of religious debates. The final one was held at the Diet of Regensburg in 1541. Calvin, the reformer from Geneva, participated; and for the first time the Jesuits were present. The latter became important exponents of the Counter-Reformation.

1534
The Reformation Takes Root Plates 123—138

In many German territories and all over Europe the Reformation seized a foothold during this time. In 1534 Wuerttemberg became evangelical. In a sober and discreet manner Johannes Brenz had worked as a preacher for the Reformation in Schwaebisch Hall since 1522. He advised and negotiated during the introduction of reform by Duke Ulrich of Wuerttemberg in this part of southern Germany.

In 1538—39 the electorate of Brandenburg became evangelical. Luther's pupil and friend, John Agricola, was made court preacher in Berlin in 1540. He directed and inspected the church in the Mark of Brandenburg.

In 1539 Duke George of Saxony died without leaving any male descendants. Now the road was paved for the evangelical church in his territory of ducal Saxony.

Luther's close friend, Nicholas von Amsdorf, became the first evangelical bishop, namely, in Naumburg from 1541 to 1547. Then he had to relinquish his position to Julius Pflug, a Catholic advocating a reform of the Roman Church; but Pflug could not forever forestall the Reformation in this region of Germany.

The Wittenberg professor, city pastor, and Luther's father confessor Johannes Bugenhagen established evangelical churches in northern Germany as well as in Denmark, using a model liturgy and regulations he had prepared for the church. The introduction of the Reformation in Denmark was not successful until the reign of the second successor to King Christian II. Christian II tried to establish the unity of the three northern states of Denmark, Norway, and Sweden through the so-called Stockholm Bloodbath, in which many Swedish noblemen died. His attempt to use the Reformation for political reasons failed, and he was driven out of Denmark. Under the rule of King Christian III the Diet of Copenhagen in 1536 established the Lutheran faith in Denmark as the state religion.

In Sweden King Gustav Vasa carried through the Reformation in 1527 with the help of Luther's pupil, Olavus Petri, and Laurentius Andreae, his widely traveled and humanistically educated co-worker. There were, naturally, political reasons behind the king's efforts to bring Lutheranism to Sweden. The Gustav Vasa Bible of 1541, translated by the two brothers, Olavus and Laurentius Petri, became important. The latter became the first evangelical archbishop of Uppsala in 1531. In Sweden the apostolic succession was retained.

These are only a few examples of how the Reformation in Europe took root. They show how similar and yet how diverse the road was in establishing the evangelical church. It is obvious that the Reformation was not always free of motives outside of the realm of religion.

In some places the newly established churches did not survive the Counter-Reformation.

Luther had remained during this time the spiritual leader of these newly established churches, or at least the spiritual adviser, but the Reformation movement had grown far beyond him.

1546

Luther's Death   Plates 139—142

Luther died on Feb. 18, 1546, working until his last days. The cause of death was probably heart failure. This is not surprising at the end of a life abounding in work, conflict, and excitement. For many years, frequent illnesses had plagued the Reformer. He suffered kidney stones, the fashionable disease of the day; attacks of weakness; and dizziness. Obviously, he suffered from circulatory problems. In addition there were numerous temporary pains. His ever-growing vehemence, and the increased sharpness of his expressions were probably the result of his physical sufferings; but above all, they can be traced to his spiritual exertions lasting for decades. It ought to be noted in this connection that the time in which Luther lived, generally speaking, was not exactly a time of prudishness.

At the close of his life, Luther used the old liturgy of dying attributed to Archbishop Anselm of Canterbury.[15] Responding to the question as to whether or not he wanted to remain steadfast to Christ and the doctrine he had preached, Luther answered in his hour of death with a distinct and clear yes.

He was buried in the Castle Church in Wittenberg, where his remains still rest untouched. When a year later Charles V stood at his grave in the course of the Schmalkaldic War, and was requested by Duke Alba to desecrate Luther's grave; the emperor, the Knight of the Golden Fleece, is said to have replied that he waged no war against the dead. Across from Luther rests Melanchthon, who outlived Luther by 14 years, freed from the bickering of the theologians which embittered the twilight of his life.

1546

Outbreak of the Schmalkaldic War   Plates 143—148

It was good for Luther that he was spared the experience of the events which were to come. After all, he had survived the papal and imperial ban; but woe to him if he should encounter the emperor a second time.

Now the military preparations which had been feared by the Protestants for a long time were in the making. Foreign policy matters became sufficiently settled to permit the emperor to move against the evangelicals. He had divided them, thanks to the diplomatic skill of his court. Philip of Hesse had played into the emperor's hands by his bigamous marriage, an act which was clearly against the laws of the empire. The emperor had recognized the indecent endeavor of Duke Moritz of Saxony, the nephew of Duke George, to obtain the electorship, and had offered him the possibility, demanding in return neutrality and imperial obedience.

In the summer of 1546 Charles announced at the Diet of Regensburg that he wanted to restore unity and peace in Germany. That was the declaration of war.

There was no decisive battle during the first phase of the Schmalkaldic War, the Danube campaign in southern Germany. When Duke Moritz of Saxony treacherously attacked the Schmalkaldic princes from the rear and invaded the electorate of Saxony, the princes were decidedly weakened and dispersed, since John Frederick hurried home to defend his threatened electorate.

Charles now moved in triumph through Swabia and reestablished monasteries and convents. Then he continued to Saxony in order to aid Duke Moritz.

There was the decisive battle at Muehlberg on the Elbe River on April 24, 1547. From the left bank of the Elbe at Schirmenitz a ford was located in the course of the river at that time. John Frederick moved with his troops toward Wittenberg or Magdeburg, heading north on the right bank of the river. The emperor and his troops approached from the left bank and attacked from the flank. After the regular Sunday morning worship, when the fog on the river lifted before midday, the elector John Frederick saw the enemy. However, he did not attempt to hold his side of the bank but rather wanted to continue his march as quickly as possible toward the north. The emperor personally witnessed his Spanish warriors capture the pontoons for the bridge of the elector and achieve the river crossing.

The battle led to a flight in which towards evening, 15 miles north of Muehlberg, John Frederick was captured. He was brought before the emperor, who personally had taken part in the last phases of the campaign. Throughout the Schmalkaldic War, Charles was afflicted with the gout, which often forced him to ride with only one foot in the stirrup.

The other important leader of the Schmalkaldic princes, Philip of Hesse, was also captured by means of deception. Only the north German cities, in particular Magdeburg and Bremen, defied the emperor. It appeared to be a complete victory for Charles V.

1548

Adiaphoristic Controversy

Plate 149

The Protestants, severely oppressed externally, now apparently wasted further strength on internal theological battles. Disunity and schism now showed itself in all its fullness.

In 1548 the emperor had attempted to settle religious questions in Augsburg on a provisional basis. The so-called *Augsburg Interim,* a temporary solution, was established. In no way was that a recognition of the evangelical faith but in fact a restoration of the old belief. To be sure, the cup was restored to the laity and the marriage of priests was permitted, but only until a decision on such questions should be reached by a church council.

These regulations, however, could be carried out only in areas of imperial influence and therefore only in southern Germany. Even here they frequently encountered passive resistance.

In central and northern Germany Elector Moritz of Saxony, with the help of Philipp Melanchthon, Julius Pflug, and the sober, pious, and evangelical George of Anhalt, who had been ordained "bishop" of Merseburg by Luther, attempted to implement a different document of mediation, the so-called *Leipzig Interim.* It contained a mixture of Catholic and evangelical elements which, if need be, permitted Protestant interpretation. The authors, however, were ready to accept the papacy, as well as many former regulations, including the seven sacraments, because these "unimportant" things, *adiaphora,* would not affect the central faith.

1548

"Philippists"

Plate 150

These adiaphora resulted in controversy. Uncompromising theologians thought the *Leipzig Interim* went too far. They declared *"nihil est adiaphoron in casu confessionis et scandali,"* "nothing is unimportant in the case of confession and scandal." Melanchthon was placed under suspicion. Did he not always maintain an interceding attitude? He even wanted to change the *Augsburg Confession* of 1530 slightly, above all, the article dealing with the Lord's Supper; and this resulted in the altered *Confessio Augustana,* the *Confessio Augustana variata* of 1540. This version of the Confession satisfied those who did not share Luther's conception of the Lord's Supper. In addition, later editions of the *Loci Communes* in the 1530s and 1540s showed that the Humanism of Melanchthon, the great scholar, educator, and church politician, had never been completely surmounted by Luther's theology. Thus, distrust and resentment increased more and more among those who considered themselves pure pupils of Luther. They set themselves apart from the "Philippists," the advocates of Melanchthon's interpretation.

1548

Gnesio-Lutherans   **Plates 151—154**

And so the "genuine Lutherans," the Gnesio-Lutherans, migrated from Wittenberg. The University of Jena was founded in 1558, and it became the center of the Gnesio-Lutherans. Its leaders were Amsdorf, and more particularly, a high-spirited theologian from Istria, Matthias Flacius, called Illyricus. During a most severe inner conflict, he found solace in justification "by grace alone." He would not—indeed could not—bring himself to detract anything from this doctrine. Lutheranism is indeed indebted to him for not suffering any loss of Luther's essential discoveries. Since, however, Flacius developed more and more into a theologian of controversy, he did not remain free from harshness and exaggerations.

Melanchthon himself later admitted that he had sinned in the adiaphoristic controversy. The quarrels, however, could not be set aside completely, because Flacius and his followers demanded a public repentance from the Wittenberg theologians.

Out of this adiaphoristic controversy immediately came additional quarrels—the majoristic, the antinomistic, and the synergistic controversies. They had their foundation in that the Philippists insisted that in addition to salvation through grace alone, *sola gratia,* justification includes personal experience and moral revival.

1548
"Good Works" and Other Controversies   Plates 155—156

The Wittenberg professor George Major had been attacked in the adiaphoristic controversy by Amsdorf on account of his thesis that good works were necessary if one wanted to obtain salvation. Flacius held that the question of a renewal of the believer's life was to be separated completely from justification. Amsdorf finally even went so far as to assert that good works were damaging with respect to obtaining salvation.

In the antinomistic controversy the problem dealt with the "third use of the Law," namely, whether the Law, as a directive to act justly, still played a role for the forgiven Christian. However, this seemed inconsistent with Luther's thesis, that man is "just and a sinner at the same time," *simul iustus, simul peccator.*

Against the opinion of John Pfeffinger, Amsdorf and Flacius maintained in the synergistic controversy that man is completely incapable of contributing anything to the obtaining of salvation. Flacius' rigidity finally led to his teaching that original sin became the substance of man through the fall of Adam.

1549
Osiander Controversy   Plate 157

Likewise, arguments in the Osiander controversy about the understanding of justification were debated. Andreas Osiander, the former reformer of Nuernberg, had to leave this city on account of the Interim and other disagreements and had gone to the newly established university in

Koenigsberg in 1549. The Controversy broke out in the open there. Osiander based the justification of man on the effective indwelling of the divine nature of Christ by the Word and faith. The work of salvation and forgiveness of sins are only prerequisites for bringing about the effective justification. The Gnesio-Lutherans, as well as the Philippists, opposed him. They both held that he minimized forgiveness and that with Osiander the speculation about belief finally results in Gnosticism. The entire church of the duchy of Prussia, the first territory to become evangelical, was torn apart by these party quarrels.

1549

Crypto-Calvinist Controversy and Further Events   Plate 158

Controversies about the Lord's Supper also split the Lutherans into factions. The Philippists were now called "Crypto-Calvinists," meaning "secret Calvinists."

In 1555, after the military victory of Duke Moritz of Saxony, against the emperor, the Lutherans were given recognition according to the laws of the empire, but only after the emperor had relinquished his rule over German affairs. This became the Religious Peace of Augsburg. By it, the right to reform, however, was given only to the territorial princes.

Soon thereafter Catholicism took on a new form, based on the decisions of the Council of Trent in 1563. The Catholic Church became more pliable because of the Reformation. The most mischievous abuses were eliminated by the council, but doctrinal positions had also been made permanent, so that the rift between Catholics and evangelicals became even deeper.

In the meantime in Switzerland, the followers of Zwingli and Calvin had united in 1549 on the basis of their agreement in Zurich about the Lord's Supper, the so-called *Consensus Tigurinus*.

TOMAS MVNZER PREDIGER ZV ALSTET IN DVRINGEN.

PLATE 92. Thomas Muenzer. Engraving by Christoph von Sichem, 1608. (Lutherhalle, Wittenberg)

PLATE 93. City of Muehlhausen. In the background the recently renovated St. Mary's Church. It now serves the community as a concert hall.

PLATE 94. One of the main portals of St. Mary's Church in Muehlhausen. Thomas Muenzer preached to the crowds that gathered from the steps of this church.

PLATE 95. The parsonage of Thomas Muenzer in Muehlhausen, in the background, is located adjacent to St. Mary's Church.

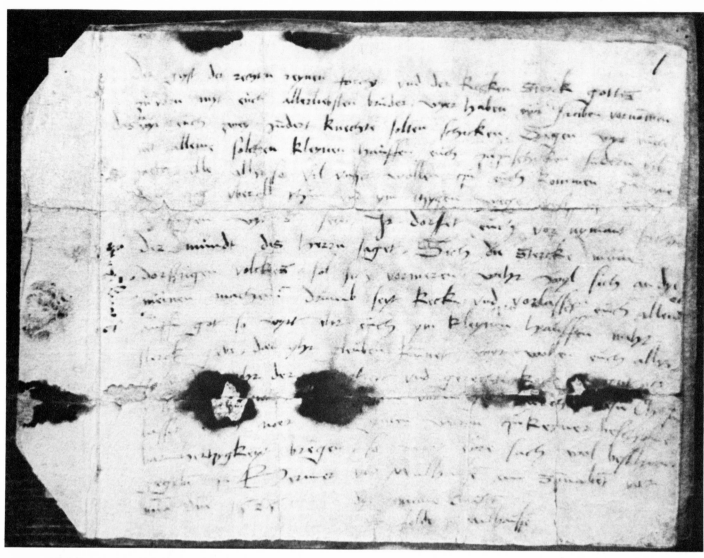

PLATE 96. An original letter by Thomas Muenzer to the parish of Frankenhausen. The letter is dated April 29, 1525. (Stadtarchiv, Muehlhausen)

PLATE 97. The elector of Saxony, John the Steadfast. Detail from a painting by an unknown artist, 16th century. In the background a representation of the battle at Frankenhausen, in which Thomas Muenzer and his followers were defeated May 15, 1525. A rainbow, a symbol of Muenzer and his followers, is shown over the battlefield. (Museum Schloss Wilhelmsburg, Schmalkalden)

wider die Mordischen

vnd Reubischen Rotten der Bawren.

Psalm. vij.
Seyne tück werden jn selbs treffen/
Vnd seyn mutwill/ wirdt vber jn außgeen.
1525.
Martinus Luther. Wittenberg.

PLATE 98. Title page of Luther's tract against the Peasants. *Against the Robbing and Murdering Hordes of Peasants*, Wittenberg, 1525. (Lutherhalle, Wittenberg)

PLATE 99. Last remnants of the Convent Nimbschen near Grimma on the Mulde River. Luther's wife, a former nun, escaped from here on the Saturday before Easter, April 7, 1523. The convent was founded in the 13th century and dissolved in 1536.

PLATE 100. Martin Luther, also called Luther's wedding portrait. Painting by Lucas Cranach the Elder, 1526. (Wartburg-Stiftung, Eisenach)

PLATE 101. Katharina von Bora, Luther's wife. Painting by Lucas Cranach the Elder, 1526. (Wartburg-Stiftung, Eisenach)

PLATE 102. "Let the Children Come to Me." The painting is said to portray Luther's children; his son Paul, lower right, his daughter Margarethe holding a child in the center of the painting. Painting by Lucas Cranach the Elder, 1529. (St. Wenzel's Church, Naumburg)

PLATE 103. Desiderius Erasmus of Rotterdam, with whom Luther took issue on the question concerning "the bondage of the will." Engraving by Albrecht Duerer, 1525. (Lutherhalle, Wittenberg)

PLATE 104. Title page of the so-called *Zwickauer Gesangsbuechlein*, 1526. It is an early church hymnal containing a number of hymns by Martin Luther. (Ratsschulbibliothek, Zwickau)

Folget eyn hubsch Euange-
lisch lied welchs mann singt
fur der Predig.

Nu frewt euch lieben Christen gemeyn/
vnd last vns frölich springen/Das wyr
getröst vnd all yn eyn/mit lust vnd liebe
singen/Was Got an vns gewendet hat/
vnd seyne susse wunder that/Gar thewr
hat ers erworben.

Dem teuffel

PLATE 105. A page from the *Zwickauer Gesangsbuechlein*, 1526. It shows Luther's first hymn, *"Nun freut euch lieben Christen gemein"* ("Dear Christians, let us now rejoice"). (Ratsschulbibliothek, Zwickau)

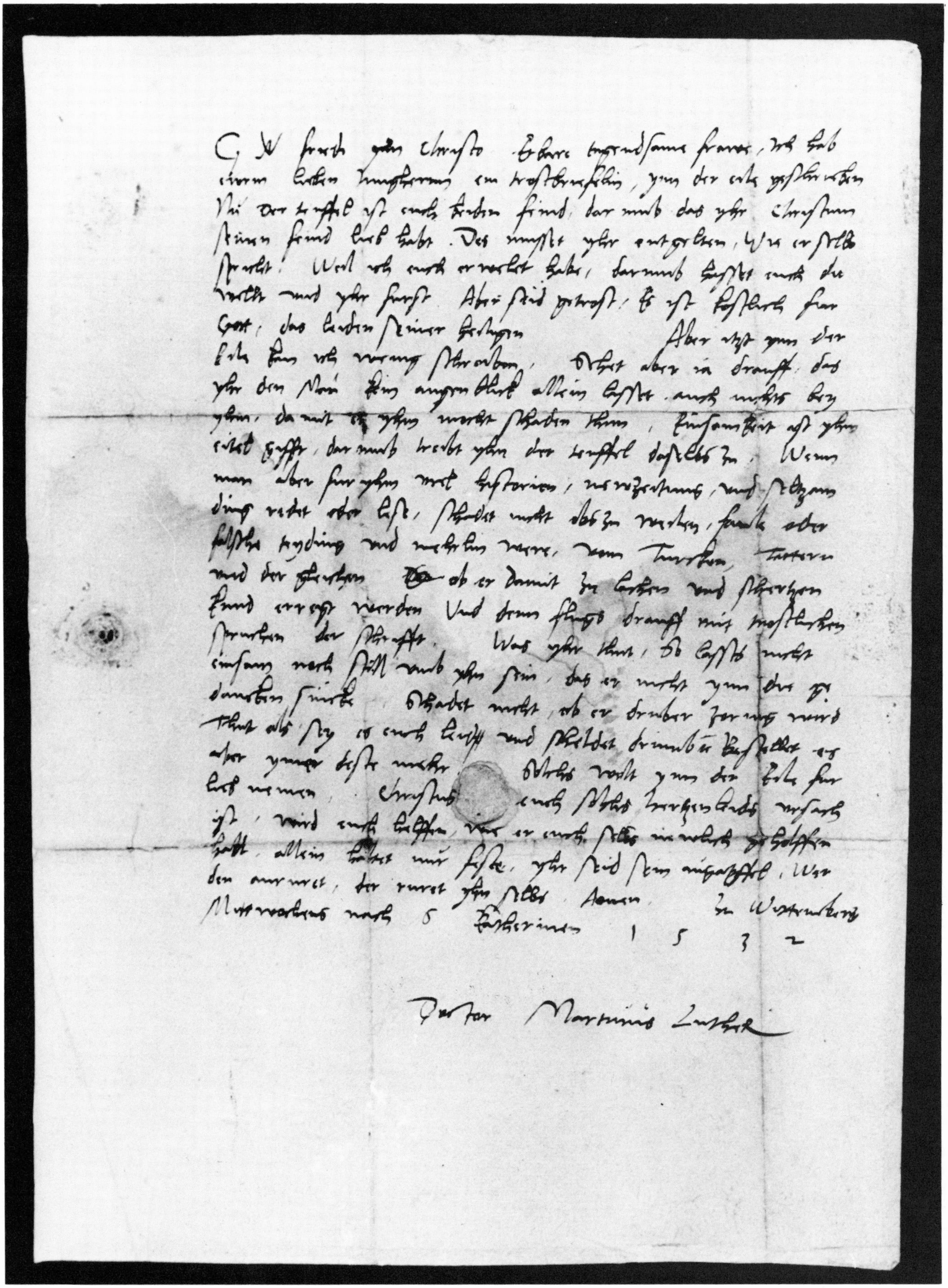

PLATE 106. An original letter by Luther to Mrs. Stockhausen, whose husband contemplated suicide, dated 1532.
(Archiv und Bibliothek des Evangelischen Ministeriums zu Erfurt)

PLATE 107. The Lord's Supper with the Reformers as the disciples of Christ. (See jacket.) Reformation Altarpiece by Lucas Cranach the Younger, 1565. (Village church in Mildensee near Dessau)

PLATE 108. Title page of Luther's tract *Confession Concerning Christ's Supper*, Wittenberg, 1528. (Augustana College Library, Rock Island, Illinois)

IESVS · MAT · XI ·

VENITE AD ME · QVI   LABORATIS · ET EGO REFICIÃ VOS ·

HVLDRICVS · ZVINGLIVS ·
ANNO ÆTATIS · 44 ·
· B ·

PLATE 109. Ulrich Zwingli. Engraving by René Boyvin after a painting by Hans Asper, 1531. (Kunstsammlungen zu Weimar)

Yn Antwurt Huld-rychs Zuinglins vff die

Epistel Joannis Pugenhag vss Pomieren/ das Nachtmal Christi betreffende.

Christus Matthei xj.
Kumend zů mir alle die arbeytend vnd bela
den sind/ vnd ich wil üch růw geben.

Getruckt zů Zürich by Christoffel
Froschouer / im jar
M. D. XXVI.

PLATE 110. Title page of Zwingli's tract *An Answer to Bugenhagen's Tract Dealing with the Lord's Supper.* Zurich, 1526. (Lutherhalle, Wittenberg)

PLATE 111. Marburg, on the Lahn River. View toward the former castle of Philip of Hesse, who invited the Wittenberg theologians, Zwingli, and others to a religious debate in 1529.

PLATE 112. Philip of Hesse. A painting attributed to Hans Krell, 1525—30. (Wartburg-Stiftung, Eisenach)

PLATE 113. City of Speyer. The diets of 1526 and 1529 took place in this city. The name "Protestants" was recorded in the minutes of the diet of 1529. It referred to the protesting evangelical princes.

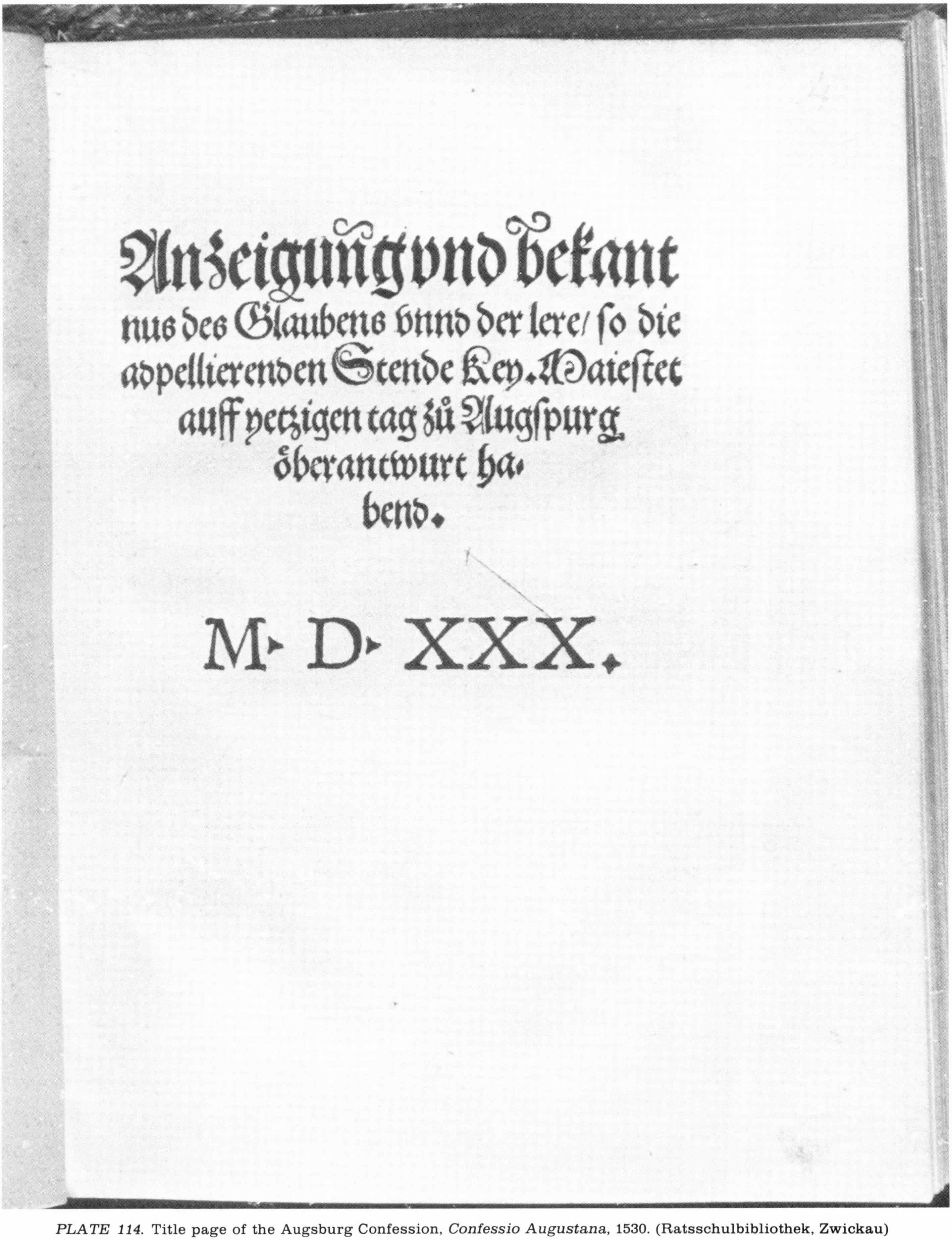

Anzeigung vnd bekant

nus des Glaubens vnnd der lere/ so die adpellierenden Stende Key. Maiestet auff yetzigen tag zů Augspurg ŏberantwurt haben.

M· D· XXX·

PLATE 114. Title page of the Augsburg Confession, *Confessio Augustana*, 1530. (Ratsschulbibliothek, Zwickau)

EFFIGIES PHIL: MELANCHTHONIS · ANN · AET ·
XXX C̄Z̄ LVCA CRONACHIO PICTORE ·
· M · D · XXXVII ·

PLATE 115. Philipp Melanchthon, who primarily drafted the *Confessio Augustana* to be presented at the Diet of Augsburg in 1530. Painting by Lucas Cranach the Younger, 1537. (Staatliche Kunsthalle, Karlsruhe)

PLATE 116. The Coburg Castle. Luther stayed here during the Diet of Augsburg in 1530, for he was under imperial ban.

PLATE 117. City of Augsburg. The imperial diet of 1530 took place in this building. The festivities were held on the first floor at the right.

PLATE 118. City of Schmalkalden. View from the Wilhelmsburg Castle toward the City Church, St. George. The Schmalkaldic League met eight times in this city between 1530 and 1534. The city, near the Thuringian Forest, dates back to 1272.

PLATE 119. Title page to the first complete German Bible. Printer Hans Lufft, Wittenberg, 1534. (Lutherhalle, Wittenberg)

PLATE 120. A page, entitled "Creation," from the first Luther Bible. Woodcut by Cranach's workshop. Printer Hans Lufft, Wittenberg, 1534. (Lutherhalle, Wittenberg)

PLATE 121. Luther House in Schmalkalden. Luther was ill when the Protestant princes came to Schmalkalden for a meeting of the league in 1537. Therefore Luther received his guests on the third floor of this building dating back to the beginning of the 16th century. Among the guests were Ulrich, duke of Wuerttemberg; Philip of Hesse; Melanchthon; Spalatin; Bugenhagen; and Justus Jonas.

PLATE 122. Regensburg, on the Danube River. An ecumenical attempt was made here to come to an agreement by means of religious debate. View toward the cathedral. The building where the diet of 1541 took place stands near the cathedral.

PLATE 123. St. Michael's Church in Schwaebisch Hall. Johannes Brenz worked here to bring the Reformation to this part of southern Germany.

IOANNES · BRENTIUS *Theologus*

Nasc. Weillw in Suecuia, Aᵒ. 1499. 24 𝘑ᵘ, Ob. Stutgardiæ Aᵒ. 1570. 20. Sept.

Ardor eras veræ brenti pietatis, illum.
Ardorem incendit Relligionis amor.

PLATE 124. Johannes Brenz. After an engraving by John Theodor de Bry, 1597. (Lutherhalle, Wittenberg)

PLATE 125. St. Mary's Church in Berlin. John Agricola worked here to bring about the Reformation in Brandenburg. He succeeded in 1563.

Natus 2 April. 1490
Denatus peste
22 Sept.
A? 1566.

28

IOHAN AGRICOLA ISLEBIVS THEOLOGVS BRANDEBVRGICVS ET GENERALIS MARCHIÆ SVPERINTENDENS.

PLATE 126. John Agricola, also called Schnitter. After an engraving by Balthasar Jenichen, 1565. (Lutherhalle, Wittenberg)

PLATE 127. City of Naumburg. View from the tower of Wenzel's Church toward the cathedral. Nicholas von Amsdorf, the first Protestant bishop, was active here and came into dispute with the Catholic bishop Julius Pflug.

PLATE 128. Nicholas von Amsdorf. Detail of his grave marker. (St. George's Church, Eisenach)

PLATE 129. Julius Pflug, Catholic bishop in Naumburg. Painting by an unknown artist at the end of the 16th century. (Museum der Stadt Naumburg, Saale)

EFFIGIES IOH BVGENHAGII POMERANI ·
LVCA CRONACHIO PICTORE ·
· M · D · X X X VII ·

PLATE 130. Johannes Bugenhagen, the reformer in northern Germany and Denmark. Painting by Lucas Cranach the Younger, 1537. (Lutherhalle, Wittenberg)

PLATE 131. Copenhagen, Denmark. View toward the building in which the diet of 1536 introduced Lutheranism as the state religion in Denmark.

PLATE 132. King of Denmark, Christian II. Painting by Lucas Cranach the Elder, 1523. (Museum der Bildende Kuenste, Leipzig)

PLATE 133. St. Nicholas Church in Copenhagen. Hans Tausen began to preach Lutheranism here in 1527.

PLATE 134. Statue of Olavus Petri, the reformer in Sweden. It is located in front of *Storkyrkan* (St. Nicholas Church) in Stockholm.

PLATE 135. City of Stockholm. *Storkyrkan* (St. Nicholas Church) is located at the far left. In the center is the tower of the German Church.

PLATE 136. Back of title page of the Swedish New Testament, 1526. Woodcut by an unknown artist, late 15th century. It illustrates Christ on the cross with John the Baptist and the Virgin Mary. Copy from the *Uppsala Missal*, 1513. This excellent woodcut was the work of one of the most important artists of the time, who signed his work "DS." (Universitet Uppsala)

SIC·REX·GVSTAVS
ROSQVE
FŒLIX·IMPERIO

VVLTV·QVE·HVME
FEREBAT:
SVECIA·MAGNATVO
1542

PLATE 137. King of Sweden, Gustav Vasa I. Painting by an unknown artist, 1542. (Universitet Uppsala)

Genesis / Första Boken Mose.

Första Capitel.

Hebre. 11
Collof. 1.
Joan. 1.

Begynnelsenn skapadhe Gudh himmel och iord. Och iorden war ödhe och toom / och mörker war på diwpet / och Gudz ande sweffde offuer watnet.

Och Gudh sadhe / Warde liws / Och thet wardt liws / Och Gudh sågh liwset at thet war gott. Tå skilde Gudh liwset ifrå mörkret / och kalladhe liwset / Dagh / och mörkret / Natt. Och wardt aff affton och morghon förste daghen.

Och Gudh sadhe / Warde itt fäste emellan watnen / och åttskilie watn ifrå watn. Och Gudh giorde fästet / och åttskilde thet watnet som war vnder fästet / ifrå thet watn / som war offuan fästet. Och thet skeedde så. Och Gudh kalladhe fästet / Himmel. Och wardt aff affton och morghon / then andre daghen.

Och Gudh sadhe / Församle sigh watnet som är vnder himmelen / vthi besynderlighit rwm / at thet torra må synas / och thet skeedde så. Och Gudh kalladhe thet torra / Jord / och watnens församlingar kalladhe han / haaff / och Gudh sågh at thet war gott.

Och Gudh sadhe / Bäre iorden grääs och örter som fröö haffua / och fruchtsam trää / at hwart och itt bäär frucht effter sijn artt / och haffuer sitt eghit fröö j sigh sielffuo på iordenne / och thet skeedde så.

Och iorden baar grääs och örter som fröö hadhe hwart effter syna artt / och trää som frucht båro / och hadhe sitt eghit fröö j sigh sielffuo / hwart effter sina artt. Och Gudh sågh at thet war gott. Och warde aff affton och morghon / then tridie daghen.

Och Gudh sadhe / Warde liws vthi himmelens fäste / och åttskilie dagh och natt / och giffue tekn / månadher / daghar och åår / och ware för liws vthi himmelens fäste / och lyse på iordena / Och thet skeedde så. Och Gudh giorde tw stoor liws itt stoort liws / som regeradhe daghen / och itt litit liws som regeradhe nattena / och stiernor. Och Gudh satte them vti himmelens fäste / at the skina skulle på iordena / och regera daghen och natena / och åttskilia liwset och mörkret. Och Gudh sågh at thet war gott. Och wardt aff affton och morghon / then fierde daghen.

A

Och

(Tekn) Såsom Soolhuaff Månas huatff och annor vnder på himmelen / Månadher / Såsom Nymånat / Fulmånat etc. Daghar / såsom påska pingest daghar etc.

PLATE 138. A page of the so-called Gustav Vasa Bible, 1541. It is the first complete Bible in the Swedish language. (Universitet Uppsala)

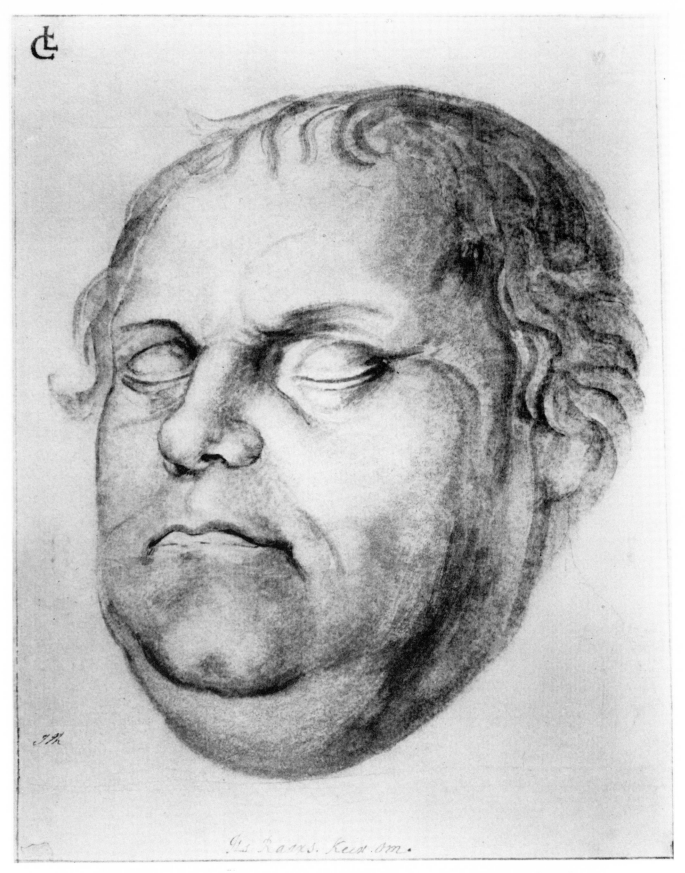

PLATE 139. Luther in death. Drawing by Lucas Furtenagel, 1546. (Lutherhalle, Wittenberg)

PLATE 140. The house in which Luther died in Eisleben, the city of his birth. View from the courtyard. It is located adjacent to St. Andrew's Church and dates back to the beginning of the 16th century.

PLATE 141. The rays of the sun strike Luther's grave in the Castle Church in Wittenberg. Luther's wife died in 1552. She lies buried in Torgau, the city to which she came when she escaped from the Convent Nimbschen almost three decades earlier.

PLATE 142. Bronze grave plate of Martin Luther by Heinrich Ziegler the Younger, 1548—49. It was cast in Erfurt and is located in the City Church, St. Michael, Jena.

PLATE 143. The village of Schirmenitz. View toward the village church. The battlefield was located behind the village church.

PLATE 144. Emperor Charles V in his later years. Painting by Lucas Cranach the Elder, ca. 1550. (Wartburg-Stiftung, Eisenach)

PLATE 145. The former headquarters of Charles V during the battle at Schirmenitz was located in the farm building at the left. It is next to the village church.

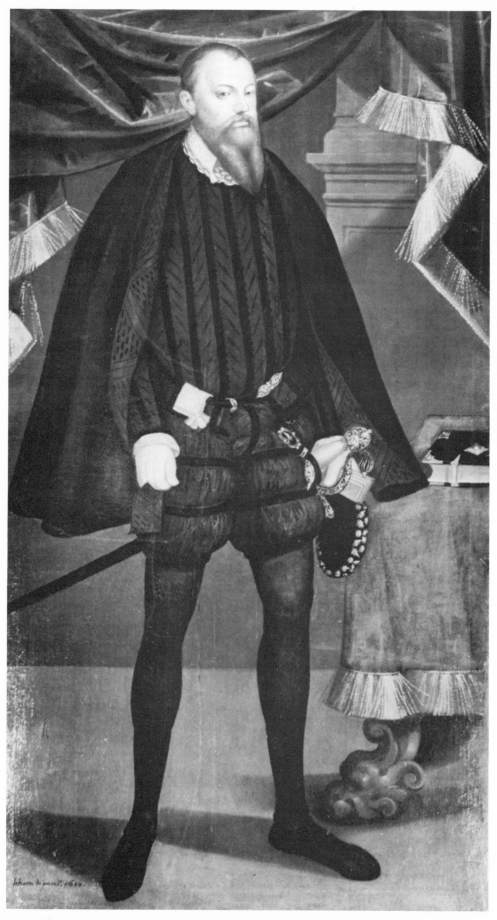

PLATE 146. Duke Moritz of Saxony, the ambitious nephew of Duke George the Bearded. Painting by John de Peere, 1616. (Museum fuer Geschichte der Stadt Leipzig)

PLATE 147. Muehlberg on the Elbe River, scene of the decisive battle on April 24, 1547, in which the Protestant Princes were defeated by the imperial forces of Emperor Charles V. View toward the former castle in Muehlberg.

PLATE 148. Elector of Saxony, John Frederick, who was captured north of Muehlberg in 1547 and brought before the emperor. Painting by Lucas Cranach the Elder, 1526. (Kunstsammlungen zu Weimar)

Confessio oder Bekentnis des Glaubens / Durch den durchleuchtigsten / hochgebornen Fürsten vnd Herrn / Herrn Johans Hertzogen zu Sachssen / Churfürsten ꝛc. vnd etliche Fürsten vnd Stedte / vberantwort Keiserlicher Maiestat / auff dem Reichstag / gehalten zu

Augspurgk / Anno
1 5 3 0.

Vnd dieser Confession Repetitio / geschrieben von wegen des Concilij zu Trident Anno 1551.

Vnd durch den durchleuchtigsten / hochgebornen Fürsten vnd Herrn / Herrn Augustum Hertzogen zu Sachssen / Churfürsten ꝛc. von wegen der Visitation itzt wider in druck verordnet / Anno
1 5 5 5.

Wittemberg.

PLATE 149. Title page of the Augsburg Confession, *Confessio Augustana invariata*, 1530. Wittenberg, 1555. (Universitaetsbibliothek, Karl-Marx-Universitaet, Leipzig)

PLATE 150. Philipp Melanchthon, after whom the "Philippists" were named, close to the end of his life. After a woodcut by Lucas Cranach the Younger, 1561. (Lutherhalle, Wittenberg)

PLATE 151. Courtyard of the *Collegium Jenense*, the old University of Jena, seat of the Gnesio-Lutherans. The new university was founded by the elector of Saxony, John Frederick, in 1558. It is known today as Friedrich-Schiller-Universitaet, Jena.

PLATE 152. City Church, St. Michael, in Jena. Interior view toward the east. The stone pulpit, from which Luther is said to have preached, is from the year 1500.

PLATE 153. Matthias Flacius Illyricus, one of the leading spokesmen for the Gnesio-Lutherans. Painting by an unknown artist from Jena between 1571 and 1573. (Kustodie, Friedrich-Schiller-Universitaet, Jena)

Chriſtliche Bekentnus

D. Matth. Flacij Illyrici von der Erbſunde / wider das Pelagianiſche vnd Sophiſtiſche Accidens / oder euſſerſte verkleinerung der Erbvngerechtigkeit / darinnen gnugſam auff die widerwertige Sophiſtereyen vnd grewliche Gedicht geantwortet wird.

Wiltu lieber Chriſt wiſſen / was doch eigentlich die Erbſünde oder böſer Schatz vnd Vrſprung alles vbels ſey / ſo höre allein Chriſtum deinen einigen Meiſter / vnd ſeinen auserwehlten Werckzeug Paulum / Matth. 6. 12. 15. Luc. 11. Johan. 3. Rom. 6. 7. 8. 2. Cor. 3. Gal. 5. Epheſ. 2. 4. vnd Coloſ. 2. 3. Die werden dir klar ſagen / Es ſey eben das böſe Steinerne Hertz / die blinde innerliche Augen der Vernunfft / vnd der gantze böſe Adam vnd böſes Fleiſch / das ſtets wider den Geiſt vnd Wort Gottes gelüſtet vnd fichtet / Ja es ſey das fürnembſte vnd edelſte Theil oder Krafft / die den gantzen Menſchen jres gefallens vernünfftiglich / oder vielmehr boshafftiglich regieret vnd allerley Vntugenden vnd böſe Werck wider Gott vnd ſein Geſetz vnd Geiſt / nicht allein in den fleiſchlichen Menſchen / ſondern auch offt in den Widergebornen ſelbſt ſtets erwecket vnd verurſachet. Dergleichen weiſet auch die gantze Heilige Schrifft gemeiniglich auff das böſe Hertz / das daſſelbige ſey der gröſte Grewel für Gott / vnd ein Vrſprung alles vbels. Vnd das iſt eben die Erbſünde / vnd nichts anders.

Anno M. D. LXXI.

PLATE 154. Title page of a writing by Matthias Flacius concerning the original sin, 1571. (Evangelisches Pfarramt St. Andreas-Nicolai, Eisleben)

PLATE 155. George Major, a Philippist and spokesman for the controversy dealing with "good works." Detail from the Reformation Altarpiece by Lucas Cranach the Younger, 1565. (Village Church in Mildensee near Dessau)

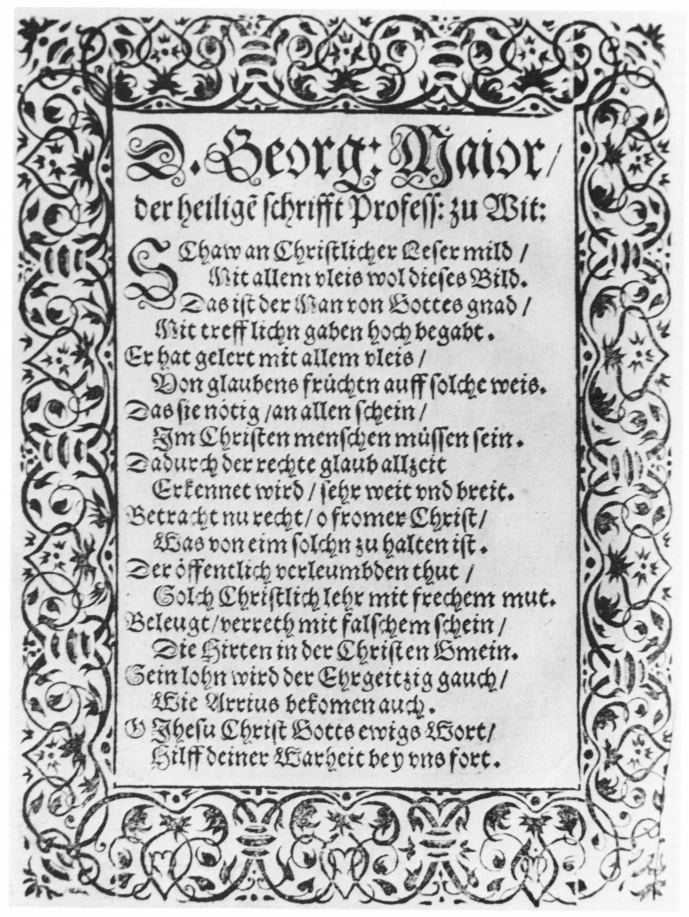

PLATE 156. A writing concerning George Major as a "true scholar and spokesman of the Holy Scripture." Printer Gabriel Schnellboltz, Wittenberg, 1562. (Universitaetsbibliothek, Karl-Marx-Universitaet, Leipzig)

ANDREAS OSIANDER

Prediger bey S. Laurenzen a. 1522.
a. 1548.

Chr. Mel. Roth. excud. Norib.

1.

PLATE 157. Andreas Osiander, who not only had the Philippists but also the Gnesio-Lutherans against him in the religious controversy concerning justification. After an engraving by Balthasar Jenichen, 1565. (Lutherhalle, Wittenberg)

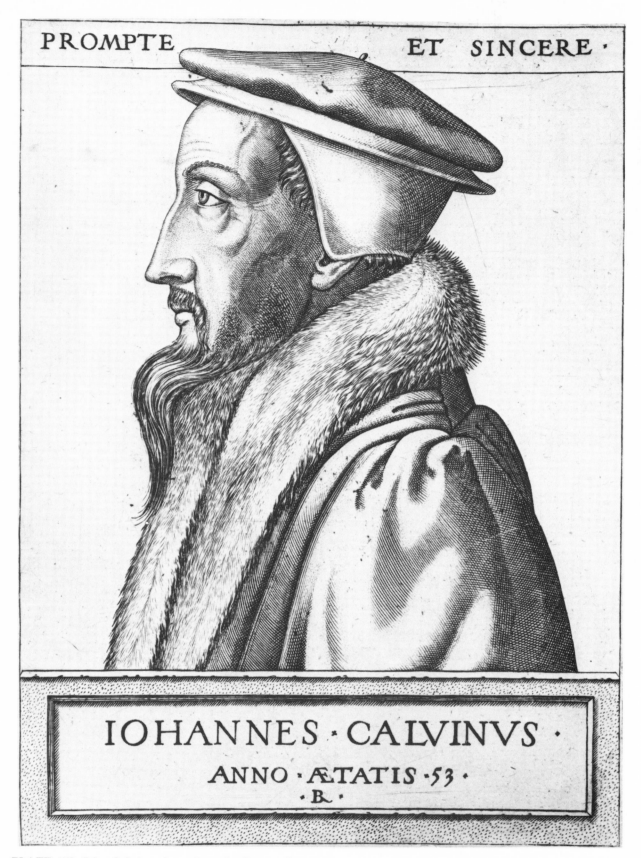

PROMPTE ET SINCERE ·

IOHANNES · CALVINVS ·
ANNO · ÆTATIS · 53 ·
· B ·

PLATE 158. John Calvin, after whom the Crypto-Calvinists were named. The name John Calvin is derived from Jean Cauvin. Engraving by René Boyvin after an old engraving. (Kunstsammlungen zu Weimar)

X. The Search for Unification and Concord, 1555–1580

1555

Peace of Augsburg and Attempt at Unification Plates 159—164

The various groups now became distinct. On the one side the Catholics stood against the Lutherans, on the other side were the Swiss. Luther had forced the Baptists and the Swiss into one camp.

Besides that there were individual opponents.

Also, there were differences enough within Lutheranism.

It was in this situation that Melanchthon died in 1560. Everything appeared to be fragmented, and so it was necessary for those to unite who were able to find unity.

Princes and theologians had been working tirelessly on that problem since the Religious Peace of Augsburg. One of the Protestant theologians laboring diligently at this task was Jakob Andreae, who had become senior pastor in 1561 and was professor and chancellor of the University in Tuebingen. Working with him towards unity were a number of important theologians, including Nicholas Selnecker, who, besides other accomplishments, was a professor in Leipzig and senior pastor of St. Thomas Church. To him we are indebted for many a hymn. Others who worked towards unity were Andreas Musculus and Christopher Cornerus, professors at Frankfort-on-the-Oder; also David Chytraeus, a teacher at the university as well as church organizer in Rostock; and Martin Chemnitz, senior pastor in the Mark Brandenburg. They were supported

by princes, among them those of Wuerttemberg, Saxony, and Brandenburg.

1577–1580

The *Formula* and *Book of Concord*   Plates 165—170

The theologians, striving towards unity, came together and held
meetings, presented formulas and confessions, traveled, collected
signatures, revised documents, and carried on negotiations. A book was
assembled in 1576 at the Hartenfels Castle in Torgau, called the *Torgau
Book.* In 1577 it was edited in the library of the former monastery Berge in
Magdeburg and bears the name *Bergic Book,* the *Formula of Concord.*

In the Formula the Lutheran doctrine is presented very thoroughly and
distinctly in the so-called *Solida Declaratio,* the thorough declaration.
Besides this there is a short summary, the *Epitome.* The signatories
separated themselves from the "papacy and all kinds of sects"; by the latter
was meant the Swiss and the radical movements of the Anabaptists. But
also they took a stand against inner-confessional deviations and errors. A
long list of signatures indicated those who approved the document.
Nevertheless, some German state churches are not listed. To the *Formula of
Concord* were added the three ecumenical Confessions and important
confessional tracts of the Reformation era. Thus, the *Book of Concord* was
evolved, and published on June 25, 1580. Those responsible had
intentionally chosen the 50th anniversary of the publication of the
Augsburg Confession, for the *Book of Concord* was supposed to be a
"genuine Christian understanding" of the *Confessio Augustana.*

With the appearance of the *Book of Concord* in 1580 the Lutheran
Church received its most thorough confessional foundation.

PLATE 159. Melanchthon grave in the Castle Church in Wittenberg. After suffering from a cold on April 4, 1560, upon his return trip to Leipzig to attend an examination of students, Melanchthon became weaker and weaker. He died on April 19, 1560.

IACOBUS ANDRÆ. THEOLOGUS ET PROFESSOR TUBINGENSIS.

PLATE 160. Jacob Andreae, theologian and professor at the University of Tuebingen. After an old engraving. (Lutherhalle, Wittenberg)

PLATE 161. Detail of the grave marker of Nicholas Selnecker. Bronze plate, end of the 16th century. (St. Thomas Church, Leipzig)

Drey Predigten
Vom heiligen Hoch=
wirdigen Abendmal vnsers
HErrn Jesu Christi.

Zu Leipzig gethan/durch

D. Nicolaum Selneccerum
Superintendenten daselbst.

Gedruckt zu Leipzig / bey
Johan Beyer / Im Jahr

M. D. LXXX.

PSALTERIVM
LATINVM DAVIDIS
PROPHETAE ET REGIS.

CVM FAMILIARI ET PIA EXPOSI-
TIONE, AC BREVI NOTATIONE ARTI-
ficii Rhetorici pertinentis ad rationem inuen-
tionis, dispositionis & elocutionis,
scripta a

Christoph. Cornero.

LIPSIÆ,
IN OFFICINA VOEGELIANA.

PLATE 163. A writing by Christopher Cornerus, 1564. (Evangelisches Pfarramt St. Andreas-Nicolai, Eisleben)

CATECHESIS
DAVIDIS CHY-
THRÆI.

POSTREMO NVNC AB
ipso Autore recognita, & multis
in locis aucta.

HALAE SAXONUM,
Typis Christophori Bismarci.
Impensis Joachimi Krusecken.
M. DC. XIII.

PLATE 164. Title page of a dogmatic writing by David Chytraeus, 1613. He was a church organizer in Rostock and worked towards unification. (Evangelisches Pfarramt St. Andreas-Nicolai, Eisleben)

PLATE 165. Hartenfels Castle in Torgau, where in 1576 the *Torgau Book* was developed. View from the east bank of the Elbe River.

PLATE 166. Interior of Hartenfels Castle in Torgau. Constructed by Nickel Grohmann. Dedicated by Martin Luther in 1544. The church was the first one built for Protestant religious services.

PLATE 167. Grosser Wendelstein, an unusual exterior spiral staircase in the courtyard of Hartenfels Castle in Torgau. The staircase was constructed by Konrad Krebs, 1536.

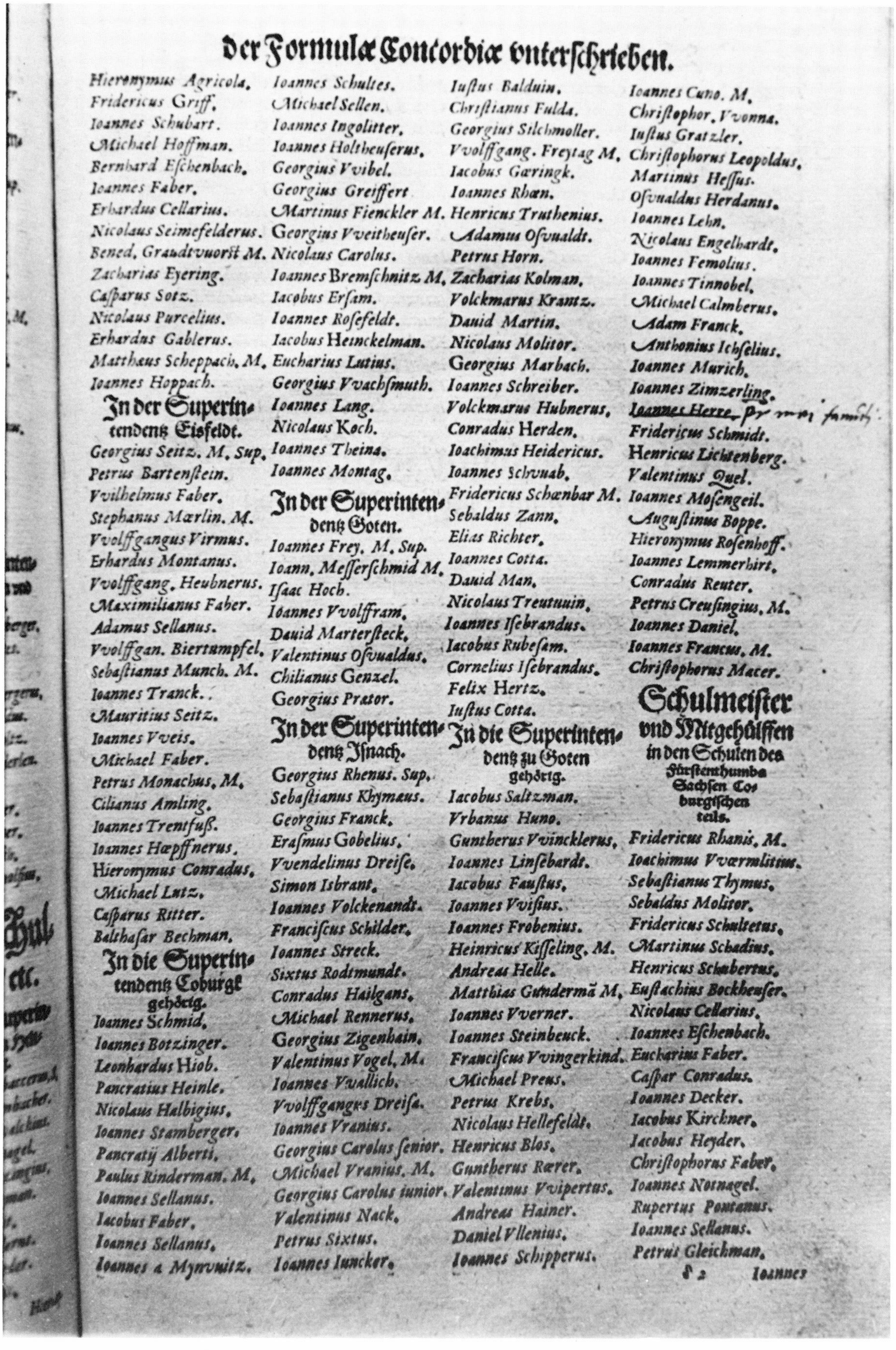

der Formulæ Concordiæ unterschrieben.

Hieronymus Agricola.
Fridericus Griff.
Ioannes Schubart.
Michael Hoffman.
Bernhard Eschenbach.
Ioannes Faber.
Erhardus Cellarius.
Nicolaus Seimefelderus.
Bened. Grandtvuorst M.
Zacharias Eyering.
Casparus Sotz.
Nicolaus Purcelius.
Erhardus Gablerus.
Matthæus Scheppach. M.
Ioannes Hoppach.

In der Superin-tendentz Eisfeldt.

Georgius Seitz. M. Sup.
Petrus Bartenstein.
Vuilhelmus Faber.
Stephanus Mærlin. M.
Vuolffgangus Virmus.
Erhardus Montanus.
Vuolffgang. Heubnerus.
Maximilianus Faber.
Adamus Sellanus.
Vuolffgan. Biertampfel.
Sebastianus Munch. M.
Ioannes Tranck.
Mauritius Seitz.
Ioannes Vueis.
Michael Faber.
Petrus Monachus. M.
Cilianus Amling.
Ioannes Trentfuß.
Ioannes Hæpffnerus.
Hieronymus Conradus.
Michael Lutz.
Casparus Ritter.
Balthasar Bechman.

In die Superin-tendentz Coburgk gehörig.

Ioannes Schmid.
Ioannes Botzinger.
Leonhardus Hiob.
Pancratius Heinle.
Nicolaus Halbigius.
Ioannes Stamberger.
Pancratij Alberti.
Paulus Rinderman. M.
Ioannes Sellanus.
Iacobus Faber.
Ioannes Sellanus.
Ioannes a Mynvnitz.

Ioannes Schultes.
Michael Sellen.
Ioannes Ingolitter.
Ioannes Holtheuserus.
Georgius Vuibel.
Georgius Greiffert.
Martinus Fienckler M.
Georgius Vueitheuser.
Nicolaus Carolus.
Ioannes Bremschnitz M.
Iacobus Ersam.
Ioannes Rosefeldt.
Iacobus Heinckelman.
Eucharius Lutius.
Georgius Vuachsmuth.
Ioannes Lang.
Nicolaus Koch.
Ioannes Theina.
Ioannes Montag.

In der Superinten-dentz Goten.

Ioannes Frey. M. Sup.
Ioann. Messerschmid M.
Isaac Hoch.
Ioannes Vuolffram.
Dauid Martersteck.
Valentinus Osvualdus.
Chilianus Genzel.
Georgius Prætor.

In der Superinten-dentz Jsnach.

Georgius Rhenus. Sup.
Sebastianus Khymæus.
Georgius Franck.
Erasmus Gobelius.
Vuendelinus Dreise.
Simon Isbrant.
Ioannes Volckenands.
Franciscus Schilder.
Ioannes Streck.
Sixtus Rodtmundt.
Conradus Hailgans.
Michael Rennerus.
Georgius Zigenhain.
Valentinus Vogel. M.
Ioannes Vuallich.
Vuolffgangus Dreisa.
Ioannes Vranius.
Georgius Carolus senior.
Michael Vranius. M.
Georgius Carolus iunior.
Valentinus Nack.
Petrus Sixtus.
Ioannes Iuncker.

Iustus Balduin.
Christianus Fulda.
Georgius Silchmoller.
Vuolffgang. Freytag M.
Iacobus Gæringk.
Ioannes Rhæn.
Henricus Truthenius.
Adamus Osvualdt.
Petrus Horn.
Zacharias Kolman.
Volckmarus Krantz.
Dauid Martin.
Nicolaus Molitor.
Georgius Marbach.
Ioannes Schreiber.
Volckmarus Hubnerus.
Conradus Herden.
Ioachimus Heidericus.
Ioannes Schvuab.
Fridericus Schænbar M.
Sebaldus Zann.
Elias Richter.
Ioannes Cotta.
Dauid Man.
Nicolaus Treutuuin.
Ioannes Isebrandus.
Iacobus Rubesam.
Cornelius Isebrandus.
Felix Hertz.
Iustus Cotta.

Jn die Superinten-dentz zu Goten gehörig.

Iacobus Saltzman.
Vrbanus Huno.
Guntherus Vuincklerus.
Ioannes Linsebardt.
Iacobus Faustus.
Ioannes Vuisius.
Ioannes Frobenius.
Heinricus Kisseling. M.
Andreas Helle.
Matthias Gundermä M.
Ioannes Vuerner.
Ioannes Steinbeuck.
Franciscus Vuingerkind.
Michael Preus.
Petrus Krebs.
Nicolaus Hellefeldt.
Henricus Blos.
Guntherus Rærer.
Valentinus Vuipertus.
Andreas Hainer.
Daniel Vllenius.
Ioannes Schipperus.

Ioannes Cuno. M.
Christophor. Vuonna.
Iustus Gratzler.
Christophorus Leopoldus.
Martinus Hessus.
Osvualdus Herdanus.
Ioannes Lehn.
Nicolaus Engelhardt.
Ioannes Femolius.
Ioannes Tinnobel.
Michael Calmberus.
Adam Franck.
Anthonius Ichselius.
Ioannes Murich.
Ioannes Zimzerling.
Ioannes Herre,
Fridericus Schmidt.
Henricus Lichtenberg.
Valentinus Quel.
Ioannes Mosengeil.
Augustinus Boppe.
Hieronymus Rosenhoff.
Ioannes Lemmerhirt.
Conradus Reuter.
Petrus Creusingius. M.
Ioannes Daniel.
Ioannes Francus. M.
Christophorus Macer.

Schulmeister und Mitgehülffen in den Schulen des Fürstenthumbs Sachsen Coburgischen teils.

Fridericus Rhanis. M.
Ioachimus Vuærmlitius.
Sebastianus Thymus.
Sebaldus Molitor.
Fridericus Schultetus.
Martinus Schadius.
Henricus Schubertus.
Eustachius Bockheuser.
Nicolaus Cellarius.
Ioannes Eschenbach.
Eucharius Faber.
Caspar Conradus.
Ioannes Decker.
Iacobus Kirchner.
Iacobus Heyder.
Christophorus Faber.
Ioannes Notnagel.
Rupertus Pontanus.
Ioannes Sellanus.
Petrus Gleichman.

8 2   Ioannes

PLATE 168. The names of some of the many who signed the *Formula of Concord*, 1577. A page from the *Book of Concord*, Dresden, 1580. (Evangelisches Pfarramt St. Andreas-Nicolai, Eisleben)

PLATE 169. Magdeburg on the Elbe River. Interior view of St. Moritz Cathedral. The *Bergic Book* of the *Formula of Concord* originated in the library of the monastery Berge, which no longer exists.

CONCORDIA.

יהוה

Christliche,

Widerholete/einmütige Bekentnüs

nachbenanter Churfürsten/ Fürsten vnd Stende
Augspurgischer Confession/ vnd derselben zu ende
des Buchs vnderschriebener Theologen
Lere vnd glaubens.

Mit angeheffter/in Gottes wort/ als der einigen Richt-
schnur/ wolgegründter erklerung etlicher Artickel/ bey
welchen nach D. Martin Luthers seligen absterben/
disputation vnd streit vorgefallen.

Aus einhelliger vergleichung vnd

beuehl obgedachter Churfürsten/ Fürsten vnd Stende/
derselben Landen/ Kirchen/ Schulen vnd Nachkommen/
zum vnderricht vnd warnung in Druck
vorfertiget.

Mit Churf. G. zu Sachsen befreihung.

Dreßden. M. D. LXXX.

PLATE 170. Title page of the *Book of Concord*, Dresden, 1580. (Evangelisches Pfarramt St. Andreas-Nicolai, Eisleben)

NOTES

1. E. G. Schwiebert, *Luther and His Times* (Concordia, 1950), p. 103. "Thus the Luthers lived in a German village with fields, meadows, water, and a common woods divided for use but owned by the entire group from generation to generation. To insure continuous succession, the estate always passed to the youngest son. The custom left the older sons free to migrate to other parts if they felt that by so doing they might improve their circumstances."

2. Pseudo-Cato, Aesop, and Terence are Greek and Roman authors whose tales are full of pranks and merriment, yet give examples for good character building.

3. Nassau was a former German dukedom from the 13th to the 19th century. Its capital was Wiesbaden.

4. E. G. Schwiebert, *Luther and His Times* (Concordia, 1950), p. 145. This Erfurt Chapter belonging to the stricter "Observantine" branch of Hermits lived according to the "Constitution by the Brothers of Hermits of St. Augustine," adopted at Nuernberg in 1504. The original Order had been founded in Italy, 1287.

5. Siegfried Hoetzel, *Luther im Augustinerkloster zu Erfurt,* 2d ed. (Berlin, 1971), p. 42. "Luther was sent by his Order to Erfurt to teach theology at the *Collegium majus,* his old university. He held his first lecture in a building next to the Cathedral *Auditorium coelicum;* all the other lectures took place in the Augustinian monastery of Hermits, where he lived and studied. We no longer know today in which room he held his lectures. We also do not know how many students came to his class."

6. The Order of the Augustinian Hermits in Europe was divided into those convents who followed the Constitution of Nuernberg in 1504, called the Observantine, for they supported the strict observance of the rules of the order, and the Conventuals, who were less rigid brothers, and opposed the Constitution. In 1507 a bull was drafted calling for union and the election of a Vicar of the Congregation. John Staupitz was reappointed vicar and provincial head of the order. Seven of the 29 Observantine convents protested the action, fearing that a union with the lax Conventuals might corrupt the entire order. This was the controversial question of organization within the order which necessitated Luther's trip to Rome.

7. The Dominicans held their chapter meeting in Rome and wanted to accuse Luther of "suspicion of heresy." He was summoned to Rome. The summons arrived in August in Wittenberg.

8. Luther said many things, for he thought he was among friends, e.g., that the papal ban did not worry him, that he was prepared to die quickly. Luther had preached a sermon on the ban in May, 1518, in the City Church in Wittenberg. A few Dominicans were in the church when Luther said that there are two kinds of Christian relationships to the church: external—that of participation in the sacraments and other outer forms—and internal, based on faith, hope, and charity. No papal ban could affect the eternal relationship between the Christian and God. The Dominicans forged a set of theses on the papal ban which they claimed were written by Luther.

9. Frederick the Wise was one of the seven who elected the emperor upon the death of Maximilian I. He was also *Reichsvikar,* who would be the interim king and rule all the eastern lands of the Holy Roman Empire. The pope needed Frederick's cooperation.

10. Cajetan was asked to place Luther under arrest if the latter did not recant. Luther's followers would also be arrested and the ban and interdict employed.

11. The wanton destruction of ecclesiastical sculptures, paintings, stained glass, etc.

12. Thomas Muenzer sought to bring the kingdom of God here on earth by force. He believed he was sent by the Holy Spirit to establish a social reform in which all class distinction was removed and all property owned communally. He wanted a new order on earth for the "elect of God" and wished to expel the unbelievers. He believed God was constantly talking to him and his followers, revealing the path in teaching and action. Muenzer had met Luther at the debate in Leipzig, and became a minister in Zwickau through Luther's influence. Here he began his radical tendencies and was expelled by the city council. He went to Prague and declared himself God's prophet of the "living Word." From there he moved to Allstedt, where he appointed himself minister of the town. Luther rejected his claim to special revelation and denounced his method by way of the sword.